Indigenous and Tribal Peoples of South America

and the International Labour Organization Convention 169

Indigenous and Tribal Peoples of South America

and the International Labour Organization Convention 169

Paulo de Bessa Antunes

Associate Profesor at Universidade Federal do Estado do Rio de Janeiro (UNIRIO). Member of the World Comission of Environmental Law - IUCN. 2019 Elisabeth Haub Environmenta Law Visiting Scholar - Pace University. Presidente of the Environmental Comitee of the Instituto dos Advogados Brasileiros.

Meraki

2022

ISBN: 978-65-88781-56-2

Acompanhamento editorial Leonam Liziero
Direção de arte Brenda Santos

Editora Meraki

A636 Antunes, Paulo de Bessa
Indigenous and Tribal Peoples of South America and the International Labour Organization Convention 169/ Paulo de Bessa Antunes. Andradina: Meraki, 2022
Bibliografia
ISBN 978-65-88781-56-2
1. Indigenous peoples 2. South America 3. International Labour Law
1. Título
CDU – 341.2:504.3 CDD – 342.087

We are not myths of the past, ruins in the jungle, or zoos. We are people and we want to be respected, not to be victims of intolerance and racism.

Rigoberta Menchú

This is dedicated to the original peoples of our
piece of the Earth, with gratitude.

Contents

Introduction

This work aims to research the judicial regime of the Constitutional Courts of South America, particularly the case law that is applicable to indigenous and tribal peoples concerning the procedure of Free, Prior and Informed Consultation stipulated in Convention 169 of the International Labour Organization - ILO. As will be demonstrated throughout this work, the construction of said case law is founded upon the following fundamental elements:

i. the historical construction of indigenist legislation[1] in the colonial period,
ii. the cultural peculiarities of indigenous peoples,
iii. the role of territory in indigenous societies,
iv. the interpretation of Convention 169 by the Inter-American Court of Human Rights, and
v. the new South American Constitutions.

Therefore, for us to address the focal point of this work, it is necessary to contextualize the theme and its numerous developments in the modern world, especially when we are dealing with the extraction of natural resources and the use of biologically diverse components that may be found within the territories occupied by indigenous and tribal peoples. Indeed it seems evident that Convention 169 and the Convention on Biological Diversity are destined to take centre stage in the continent's constitutional discussions for the next years, since Biotechnology is one of the frontiers of modern science and so-called associated traditional knowledge has become more and more relevant in the context of the pharmaceutical industry and intellectual property

[1] Indigenist Law is the law produced by a certain society to discipline the relationship with indigenous peoples. Indigenous Law is the common law of each indigenous people.

rights. When it comes to the extractivist industry, indigenous peoples have always been involved in complex issues. The difference is that today indigenous peoples occupy a juridical position never before imagined.

Indigenous and tribal peoples have increasingly been claiming their rights before national and international courts, obtaining significant successes. In fact, nowadays there is a broad assortment of case law spread across the most varied countries such as Canada, New Zealand, Australia, Papua New Guinea, and especially in Latin American countries, particularly South American countries.

The choice to study the case law of South American Constitutional Courts comes from a pragmatic decision in the face of the huge amount of research material, and the importance that such case law has been gaining.

The matter to be examined is with no doubt at the frontier of modern judicial knowledge, for it encompasses hugely different themes that intermingle in a quite complex manner. Effectively, issues that are related to International Law, Human Rights, Constitutional Rights, History, Anthropology, and many others inexorably permeate the matter, which makes the decisions true exercises of deliberation among rights that are apparently in conflict and need to be harmonized.

For the above reasons, the interdisciplinarity of the theme demands the research to be comprehensive, starting with a historical perspective of indigenist legislation, especially related to land, that advances up to the full emergence of indigenous and tribal peoples in an autonomous manner in the judicial world, as is the case with Convention 169.

The constitutional case law related to Consultation stipulated in Convention 169 is one more step in the century-long struggle of indigenous and tribal peoples for the recognition of their rights and dignity. This is what this research aims to demonstrate.

The work is arranged into 7 (seven) chapters that seek to establish a context that will allow the reader to understand the great importance of constitutional jurisprudence related to Free, Prior and Informed Consultation for indigenous and tribal peoples.

Chapter 1 is an introductory chapter that aims to present indigenist law, dividing itself into the examination of constitutional legislation and ordinary legislation, with an emphasis on the judicial regime of indigenous peoples lands. The chapter also intends to demonstrate that Free, Prior and Informed Consultation and its intention to seek agreement with indigenous peoples is a modern element, however, as we aim to demonstrate, not unprecedented, as indigenous peoples have not been passive spectators of colonization and, in one way or another, formed alliances with colonizers - Frenchmen, Spaniards, or the Portuguese, depending on each case - against enemy indigenous peoples. Thus, the major modifications relate to the prior and free character of the Consultation.

Chapter 2 will offer a broad presentation of the idea of Consultation and Free, Prior and Informed Consent as it appears in diverse international records, especially in Convention 169. We will see that the concept is not always uniform, it varies depending on the international record. There is, however, a clear tendency for increased participation of the affected communities regarding decisions about investments or projects that may impact their way of life. The theme is of such importance that there are constitutions in South America that expressively contain the provision of Consultation with indigenous peoples.

Chapter 3 is dedicated to the relations among public and private financial organizations and indigenous and tribal peoples, because of the growing concern of these institutions with indigenous issues. Due to a series of protests and criticisms, financial institutions started adopting measures to their credit policies that can assure a minimum degree of respect to human rights in projects that are carried out in indigenous lands. It goes without saying that this deals with a most relevant theme, with great and direct repercussions in the lives of indigenous peoples.

As we can see, the first three chapters lay the foundations for the subsequent chapters, which will deal more directly with the fundamental content of the research.

Chapter 4 presents the list of the communities protected by Convention 169. It is interesting to observe that in South America the only country that claims to have no indigenous or tribal peoples in its population is Uruguay, even though this allegation is widely disputable and disputed. Due to this 'nonexistence' of indigenous or tribal peoples in its population, Uruguay is not a signatory of Convention 169 and, accordingly, its Constitution does not mention the subject at all.

Chapter 5 tells us about the Brazilian communities that are fostered and protected by ILO Convention 169.

Chapter 6 offers a view on the current case law of the Inter-American system for the protection of human rights, whose repercussions for South American Constitutional Courts are more than evident. It is worth noticing, particularly, the itemization made in the framework of the system related to the conditions for making a Consultation.

Chapter 7 gives us a broad view of the decisions of several Constitutional Courts, and we have sought out the most recent and significant ones regarding Consultation. By reading different decisions it can be observed that in most countries Convention 169 has been treated as a norm that ensures fundamental human rights and has constitutional status. In the same way, these Courts have understood that Consultation has clear limits regarding its capacity to bind together the State and Public Administration, not to be mistaken for power of veto. Therefore, there is a distinction to be made between Consultation and Consent, and a need to flexibilize the application of Convention 169, as it actually follows from the text of the Constitution itself. This chapter gives particular attention to Brazil.

As for methodology, the work was carried out through bibliographic research that expanded to many areas, including Law, History, and Anthropology, among others. As for doctrine, the work sought to consult the most relevant specific doctrine, though it should be mentioned that it was found dispersed in extremely varied documents such as books, commission reports, etc. Case law research was an important instrument, and in the bibliographical references there is a list of websites where one can easily find the original texts of the decisions that are quoted and/or transcribed, partially or in full. Any international and national legislation mentioned can also be found in the list of websites in the bibliographical references.

CHAPTER 1

Evolution of Brazilian legislation about indigenous peoples and lands (Indigenist Law)

Introduction

The presence of European colonizers on the American continent immediately resulted in the existence of a set of European judicial norms that were applicable to the indigenous peoples inhabiting the New World. Such norms were not to be mistaken for the customary law existing among the various indigenous peoples. Soon, multiple rights started to coexist on the same territory, a phenomenon that caused no antagonism since judicial pluralism was only 'defeated' in the eighteenth century with the prevalence of a single and unified state law. The common law of indigenous societies is not an object of study of this work. The common indigenous law that existed in Brazil at the start of colonization, and that somehow continues to exist until today, had no major influence on the formation of Brazilian law, although it has been recognized by national law, as established by Article 231 of the Federal Constitution.[2]

[2] Article 231. Indians shall have their social organization, customs, languages, creeds and traditions recognized, as well as their original rights to the lands they traditionally occupy, it being incumbent upon the Union to demarcate them, protect and ensure respect for all of their property.Paragraph 1. Lands traditionally occupied by Indians are those on which they live on a permanent basis, those used for their productive activities, those indispensable to the preservation of the environmental resources necessary for their well-being and for their physical and cultural reproduction, according to their uses, customs and

It is notable that there is an international tendency, above all in countries with a tradition of Common Law, to find that European law did not revoke common indigenous law, except when expressly mentioned in a circumstance. The international leading case is known as the Mabo Case, that was tried in Australia and is related to the Meriam people,[3] an aboriginal group that claim rights to the Murray Islands, located in the Torres Strait. According to legal understanding prior to the case, the Murray Islands were *terra nullius*, because the Aboriginals had no consolidated concept of property rights. The arrival of the English to Australia in 1788 had established that all Australian lands became integrated as property of the British Crown. The decision on the Mabo Case (1) was declared by the Australian Supreme Court, which stated that Australian lands were not *terra nullius* before the arrival

traditions.Paragraph 2. The lands traditionally occupied by Indians are intended for their per-manent possession and they shall have the exclusive usufruct of the riches of the soil, the rivers and the lakes existing therein.Paragraph 3. Hydric resources, including energetic potentials, may only be exploit-ed, and mineral riches in Indian land may only be prospected and mined with the au-thorization of the National Congress, after hearing the communities involved, and the participation in the results of such mining shall be ensured to them, as set forth by law.Paragraph 4. The lands referred to in this article are inalienable and indisposable and the rights thereto are not subject to limitation.
Article 232, caput181Paragraph 5. The removal of Indian groups from their lands is forbidden, except ad referendum of the National Congress, in case of a catastrophe or an epidemic which rep-resents a risk to their population, or in the interest of the sovereignty of the country, after decision by the National Congress, it being guaranteed that, under any circumstances, the return shall be immediate as soon as the risk ceases.Paragraph 6. Acts with a view to occupation, domain and possession of the lands referred to in this article or to the exploitation of the natural riches of the soil, rivers and lakes existing therein, are null and void, producing no legal effects, except in case of relevant public interest of the Union, as provided by a supplementary law and such nullity and voidness shall not create a right to indemnity or to sue the Union, except in what concerns improvements derived from occupation in good faith, in the manner prescribed by law.Paragraph 7. The provisions of article 174, paragraphs 3 and 4, shall not apply to Indian lands.Article 232. The Indians, their communities and organizations have standing under the law to sue to defend their rights and interests, the Public Prosecution intervening in all the procedural acts. http://www.stf.jus.br/arquivo/cms/legislacaoConstituicao/anexo/brazil_federal_constitut ion.pdf , visited 05/13/2020

[3] Indigenist Law is the law produced by a certain society to discipline the relationship with indigenous peoples. Indigenous Law is the common law of each indigenous people.

of English colonizers. Therefore, they did not belong to anyone and the Meriam people were their rightful owners. With the Mabo Case (2), the Australian Supreme Court established the doctrine of native title deed and recognized that the Aboriginals had been expropriated from their lands.

As such, what will be examined in this part of this work is the so-called indigenist law, that is, the law intended for the indigenous peoples, but the result of a production external to indigenous societies. For our purposes, we consider the presence of Europeans in American lands *after* 1492, since the incursions by the Nordics in the region of modern Canada had a small impact on this work's theme.[4]

This chapter seeks to offer the reader a minimum outline of the complex history of the relations between Europeans and autochthonous peoples in the New World, especially regarding the legal aspects related to the personal status of indigenous peoples and their territories. The colonization of the Americas by the Iberian states had a strong religious component, though it was not limited to that. It is important to remember that the expansion to the Americas had a judicial basis in the emission of several papal documents that legitimized the enterprise from a legal standpoint. According to Adriano Moreira,[5] the Supreme Pontiff's doctrine of indirect power over earthly matters was the legal theological basis for the Iberian expansion towards the New World. The doctrine was materialized in a set of legal diplomas, such as (i) the *Romanus Pontifex* bull, 8 January 1454, Pope Nicholas V, (ii) the *Aeterni regis clementia* bull, 21 June 1481, Pope Sixtus IV, (iii) the *Inter Coetera* bull, 4 May 1493, Pope Alexander VI, (iv) the *Ea quae pro bono pacis* bull, 24 November 1506, Pope Julius II. These two last papal bulls recognized the Treaty of Tordesillas, signed by Portugal and Spain. Regarding the effectiveness of papal bulls, there is the renowned statement of Francis I, King of France: "The sun shines for me as it does for others. I would very much like to see the clause of Adam's will that divides the world

[4] http://www.newworldencyclopedia.org/entry/Leif_Ericson, Accessed on 15/10/2017.

[5] MOREIRA, Adriano. **Tratado de Tordesilhas de 7 de junho de 1494**, in, Nação e Defesa, 19th year, no. 70, April - June of 1994, Instituto de Defesa Nacional, Lisbon, pp. 9 -25.

among the Portuguese and the Spanish," referring to the Treaty of Tordesillas that was signed in 1494 to pacify disputes related to papal bulls. We must particularly note that at the start of colonization it wasn't clear yet whether Brazil would be incorporated into the Portuguese or the French colonial empire. Portuguese domination was only consolidated with the founding of the city of São Sebastião of Rio de Janeiro in 1565.

Regarding Brazil, the Society of Jesus played an essential role both in spiritual and temporal matters.[6] The whole colonizing epic raised important debates about the value of military conquests for evangelization, generating questions related to (i) just wars, (ii) the maintenance of property and equality among human beings. It is also in the same historical period that a new conception of Natural Law[7] flourished and the foundations of the emerging International Law were laid.

When the Europeans arrived, they encountered people that were totally different from those they were used to have contact with. That led to numerous theological, philosophical and political discussions among Iberian religious practitioners, especially in the writings of Friar Francisco Vitória, Friar Bartolomé de las Casas, and of Juan Ginés de Sepúlveda, the last two being the protagonists of the 'Valladolid Controversy'. The heart of the debates was the issue of how to approach the first peoples of the continent and how to integrate them, as well as their territories, with Christianity (spiritual domination) and European States (temporal domination). At the heart of those questions was the problem of the free and conscious will manifestation in accepting European domination. The matter of difference or alterity was therefore

[6] ALMEIDA, Maria Regina Celestino de. Catequese, **Aldeamentos e Missionação**, in, FRAGOSO, João and GOUVEA, Maria de Fátima (editors), **Coleção Brasil Colônia, I (1443-1580)**. 2014, p. 428.

[7] https://plato.stanford.edu/archives/sum2010/entries/colonialism, Accessed on 12/08/2017.

introduced in the European intellectual environment of colonization[8] and still remains present, despite more than 500 years of contact.

As we know, free choice is one of the central elements of Christian catechism, compulsory evangelization is not admissible. As such, it could not be disputed, from a theoretical standpoint, that indigenous consent for evangelization and also for the occupation of their lands was fundamental, thus also a factor of legitimacy. However, we must take into consideration that in two generations time the Taíno people were extinct on Hispaniola island, in Cuba, in Porto Rico, and in Jamaica.[9]

The arrival of the Europeans in America in the sixteenth century is a fact whose repercussions are still felt. Nevertheless, we mustn't be fooled by the generic designation – 'indians' – attributed to the original inhabitants of the New World. In the same way, we cannot suppose that America was subjected to *generic* Europeans. In effect, the autochthonous populations had and still have great cultural differences among them, just as the Europeans do. For that reason, there were important differences in the models of colonization of (i) Spaniards, (ii) Frenchmen, and (iii) Portuguese regarding the relationship with the native population. From the nineteenth century onwards, a process of classification and categorization of knowledge began which, regarding the relations with autochthonous populations, gave rise to a process of 'racialization'[10] of the relationship between indigenous peoples and colonizers, and later with the nation states when the independence of many former colonies took place. These relationships, however, have always been marked by ambiguity because, depending on the degree of 'friendship' or 'enmity', the indigenous peoples could be either meek or savage, which resulted in a change in their status for the Europeans.

[8] ROULAN, Norbert (editor), PIERRÉ-CAPS, Stéphanie and POUMARÈDE, Jacques. **Direito das minorias e Povos Autóctones** (Translation Ane Lize Spaltemberg). Brasília: Unb, 2004, *passim*.

[9] BACCI, Massimo Livi. **Conquista – A destruição dos Índios Americanos**. (Translation Sandra Escobar). Lisbon: Edições 70. 2007, pg. 36.

[10] BANTON, Michael. **A Ideia de Raça** (Translation António Marques Bessa), Lisbon: Edições 70, 2015. *Passim*.

> – I know what you would say; I don't share the ideas propagated among my fellows; for me the Indians, when they attack us, they are enemies to be battled; when they respect us they are vassals of a land we have conquered, but they are men!
>
> – There is no doubt, said D. Antonio de Mariz, that in his blind devotion to Cecilia he sought to gratify her wish at the risk of his life. To me one of the most admirable things that I have seen in this country is the character of this Indian. From the first day that he entered here, after rescuing my daughter, his life has been a single act of self-denial and heroism. Believe me, Alvaro, he is a Portuguese cavalier in the body of a savage."[11]

When the Portuguese settled in Brazil they encountered a large population completely installed that reminded them of Edenic myths.[12] The original peoples were not uniform and had their rivalries and controversies, which made some of them allies of the Europeans because of a pre-existing set of rivalries among the indigenous or because of concrete advantages offered by the Portuguese, the French, or the Spanish, depending on each case. Gandavo already called our attention to the importance of dissent among the indigenous peoples as a factor of Lusitanian power, "because if not for this, the Portuguese couldn't be living on the land".[13]

The modern use of the terms "autochthonous peoples" or "indigenous peoples" encompasses a great variety of social groups, such as the Tuareg, the Yanomami and the Inuit.[14] So, it seems clear that there is no consensual definition of which characteristics are sufficient to recognize a population as being autochthonous or indigenous.

[11] ALENCAR, José. **O Guarani**, in, http://www.dominiopublico.gov.br/download/texto/bv000135.pdf, Accessed on 25/11/2017.

[12] CUNHA, Manuela Carneiro da. **Índios no Brasil (História, Direitos e Cidadania)**, São Paulo: Claro Enigma, 2012. p. 8.

[13] GANDAVO, Pedro de Magalhães. **Tratado da Terra do Brasil e a História da Província de Santa Cruz**, Kindle Edition, 1574 (2014), position 305.

[14] DEROCHE, Frédéric. **La Notion de "peuples autochtones, une synthèse des principaux débats terminologiques**, in, FRITZ, Jean Claude; DEROCHE, Frédéric; FRITZ, Gérard and PORTEILLA, Raphäel (editors). **La Nouvelle Question Indigène**. Paris: L`Harmattan, 2005. p. 47

Nevertheless, it seems clear that autochthonous or indigenous are designations that stem from the concept that the centre of relations lays in those who arrived to the new place and there - to their amazement - faced the *unexpected*, the existence of populations different from the adventists. In this respect, Convention 169 is innovative because it places one of the main definitions of indigenous or tribal peoples with the very same populations it protects, which is an important alteration in the model that was in effect until then.

On the American continent - of central interest to this work - who were the autochthonous or indigenous? Initially, let us remember that the Americas were occupied from Alaska to Patagonia by numerous peoples and communities, displaying very different levels of political, economic, and social activities, with cities that were among the largest in the world at the time. Nowadays it is nothing new to recognize that these peoples had developed complex local and regional relations, with an intense exchange of information and products among them. We know that the current state of the Amazon, for example, is the result of complex ecological, geological, and human interactions,[15] which discredits the theories of an untouched nature without humans.[16]

The exact population of the Americas is unknown, there is a huge variation in the numbers, but surely there were over a few tens of millions of people.[17] As for Brazil, there were no more than five million individuals, composed by a great number of ethnies, many of whom have disappeared.[18] The most detailed information we have concerns

[15] WITKOSKI, Antonio Carlos. **Terras, Florestas e Águas de Trabalho**. São Paulo: Annablume, 2nd edition, undated. Passim.

[16] MORAN, Emilio. **Nós e a Natureza** (Translation Carlos Szlak), São Paulo: SENAC. 2008. Passim.

[17] OLIVEIRA, João Pacheco de. **Os indígenas na fundação da colônia**, in, FRAGOSO, João and GOUVEA, Maria de Fátima (editors), **Coleção Brasil Colônia, I (1443-1580)**. 2014. p. 176.

[18] ALMEIDA, Maria Regina Celestino de. **Os Índios na História do Brasil**, Rio de Janeiro: Fundação Getúlio Vargas, 2010. p. 29.

the Tupis, because they kept a more frequent and close contact with the Portuguese, be it as allies or as enemies.[19]

The contact with the Tupis was decisive for the definition of a relational pattern with the different ethnic groups. This way, the expression 'tapuia', barbarian in Tupis, came to be used to identify not only the enemies of the Tupis, but also the enemies of the Portuguese. They were tongue-tied people, incomprehensible. As far as indigenous languages are concerned, it is worth recalling Gandavo's famous passage: "The language of these gentiles all along the coast is one; it lacks three letters, [namely], you can find neither F, nor L, nor R, something rather astounding, thus they have no Faith, nor Law, nor Ruler; so they live without justice in a disorderly manner".[20] As colonization took hold, the indigenous peoples were divided into (i) 'meek indians' - those who maintained peaceful relations, or at the very least a reciprocal tolerance towards the Europeans (Portuguese) - and (ii) 'raging ones', those who resisted to colonization the longest, or who maintained alliances with other Europeans, the French, for example. The existence of 'raging indians' extended from the sixteenth to the nineteenth. Among the 'angry indians' that deserve a special mention are the ethnic groups of Caetés, Potiguaras, Goitacazes and Aimorés, who from the eighteenth century on were called *botocudos*.[21] It is curious to observe the term *desbravar* [deraging]:

> These numbers are explained in our history of *desbravamento*, that still doesn't seem to be over. *Desbravar*, a term created from indigenous blood meant "to remove the *bravos* [raging ones] during the Brazilian territorial occupation. The *bravos*, the indians, were treated as part of the territory that had to be dealt with, occupied, cleaned. 'Deforesting' and 'Deraging' characterize the manner in

[19] HOLANDA, Sérgio Buarque de. **História Geral da Civilização Brasileira - Tomo I A Época Colonial, Volume I Do Descobrimento à Expansão territorial**, Rio de Janeiro: Bertrand Brasil, 13th edition, 2003. pg. 83.

[20] GANDAVO, Pedro de Magalhães. **Tratado da Terra do Brasil e a História da Província de Santa Cruz**, Kindle Edition, 1574 (2014), position 523.

[21] ALMEIDA, Maria Regina Celestino de. **Os Índios na História do Brasil**, Rio de Janeiro: Fundação Getúlio Vargas, 2010. p. 47.

which Brazilian territory was – and to some extent continues to be – created.[22]

The relationships between settlers and indigenous peoples have always been ambiguous. We must not forget that until the consolidation of Portuguese rule – especially with the founding of the city of Rio de Janeiro in 1565 –, the French and the Portuguese kept relations with the indigenous peoples through marriages and family alliances. This is because at the start of colonization the indigenous peoples were taken for 'autonomous' nations.[23] A good example of alliance politics is the marriage of Jeronimo de Albuquerque with the daughter of Chief Arcoverde, thus uniting Portuguese and Tabajaras. It should be noted that the indigenous peoples also knew how to make the most of the divergences between the settlers, as in the renowned case of the Potiguaras, who divided themselves in support of the Dutch and the Portuguese. The complex relations between indigenous peoples and the Portuguese were the subject of a special comprehensive legislation, that we will briefly examine here.

The native peoples who were here became known as 'indians'. This designation became valid for all peoples and individuals living here. The superficiality of this generalization goes without saying. This designation, as we know, is quite misleading, since no resemblance can be claimed between the original inhabitants of our land and the populations of the Indian subcontinent. This, however, was the designation adopted for all native peoples of the 'New World'.

The 'indians', in fact, were and are constituted by diverse peoples and nations, with specific and different customs and peculiarities. They cannot be grouped into a single category. Little is known about the peoples who inhabited Brazil at the time of the colonizers' arrival. The Tupis form the best known group, because, due to the fights and wars with them, the Portuguese began to take notes on their most important

[22] NISKIER, Gustavo. **Conflitos indígenas e projetos de desenvolvimento econômico.** Master's dissertation. PUC/RJ, p. 18, in http://www.urb.puc-rio.br/dissertacao/dissertacao_gustavo_niskier.pdf, Accessed on 25/11/2017.

[23] CUNHA, Manuela Carneiro da. **Índios no Brasil (História, Direitos e Cidadania),** São Paulo: Claro Enigma, 2012. p 114.

features, etc. Other than stated by official history, colonization was not carried out without blood or fight. The disparity between the armed forces, at the organizational level, and other circumstances led the native people to be defeated before the colonizer. It is important to point out, nonetheless, that: "within the limits of their possibilities, they were tough and terrible enemies who bravely fought for their lands, safety, and freedom, that were altogether being seized from them".[24] There is no history of indigenous resistance though. History is always the history of winners, of their 'deeds'. The historiographical movement towards the 'other' side of history is recent and slight. The indigenous peoples dedicated themselves to hunting, fishing, forestry, and picking. The instruments used for their activities were generally made of rocks or wood. Iron and bronze were not known by the primitive inhabitants of Brazil.

From the beginning native Brazilians have suffered enslavement by part of the colonizers who landed here. In fact, the enslavement of gentiles' went hand in hand with the occupation of Brazilian territory, and cannot be separated from it. According to Rodolfo Garcia: "since the first contact with the land of Brazil, as it was called soon afterwards, and with the aboriginal population the discoverers started to practice slavery."[25]

The most recent historiography[26] informs us that indigenous peoples played an active role in the colony, not being mere passive spectators of colonization. A complex political game between Europeans and indigenous peoples – at times allies, other times enemies – developed throughout the whole colonization period and certainly is still developed between indigenous peoples and the modern nation states.

[24] HOLANDA, Sérgio Buarque de. **História Geral da Civilização Brasileira, 1 – A época colonial (do descobrimento à expansão territorial).** São Paulo: DIFEL, 7th edition, 1985. p. 72.

[25] GARCIA, Rodolfo. **Ensaio sobre a História Política e Administrativa do Brasil (1500-1810).** Rio de Janeiro: José Olympio/INL, 2nd edition. 1975. p. 63.

[26] For example: ALMEIDA, Maria Regina Celestino de. **Os Índios na História do Brasil**, Rio de Janeiro: Fundação Getúlio Vargas, 2010. Passim; and CUNHA, Manuela Carneiro da. **Índios no Brasil (História, Direitos e Cidadania)**, São Paulo: Claro Enigma, 2012. Passim.

Contrary to what is imagined by the lines of thought more related to Malthusian and catastrophic views of the world,[27] despite all the difficulties, indigenous peoples do not live in a state of 'collapse',[28] their population growth is very consistent.

1 Legislation applicable to the indigenous peoples in Brazil (Indigenist Law)

1.1 Common Legislation

The first set of legal norms applicable to Brazil is part of the Statute of Governor-General Tomé de Sousa,[29] with very precise determinations so that the colonial authority could exploit the rivalries and divergences between different indigenous peoples. In the same way, it included commands for the Lusitanian army to mercilessly destroy those opposed to colonization. It should be pointed out how the word 'peace' is repeated over and over in the Statute, which demonstrated the prevailing belligerent situation among settlers and indigenous peoples.

> And when such a fence is repaired and your needs are provided for, and the time seems appropriate for it, thou shalt practice, with those you understand, the way you can punish the culprits, for your safety, and with the least possible risk to us, and as you have practiced such, you shall put them in order, destroying their villages and settlements, and killing and captivating that part or them which seems enough for their punishment and sets an example to all, from then on, when they ask for peace, you shall grant it to them, forgiving them; however, it is up to them to recognize servitude and vassalage, and with the inconvenience of each year providing some provisions for the people in the settlement; and the moment they ask you for

[27] DIAMOND, Jared. **Colapso – Como as Sociedades Escolhem o Fracasso ou o Sucesso** (Translation Alexandre Raposo). Rio de Janeiro: Record, 2005, passim.

[28] McANANY, Patricia A. and YOFFEE, Norman (editors). **Questioning Collapse – Human Resilience, Ecological Vulnerability, and the Aftermath of Empire**. New York: Cambridge University Press, 2012, passim.

[29]http://lemad.fflch.usp.br/sites/lemad.fflch.usp.br/files/1.3._Regimento_que_levou_Tom__de_Souza_0.pdf. Accessed on 12/11/2017.

> peace, you shall work to have in your power some of the principal ones who were in that uprising, and those you shall order, for justice, to be hanged in the village where they were leaders.

The same Statute also carried guidelines for the evangelization of the indigenous peoples, which, in their own terms, was the 'main purpose' for the settlement on the new lands. Izidoro Martins Junior[30] highlights the fact that even the noble ones who really desired the dissemination of faith did not prevent the Statute from establishing expulsion, captivity, and death as sanctions and exemplary punishment for those who did not accept colonial peace. In the project of colonization, as we can see, there was no room for complacency or tolerance for the primitive occupiers of our Brazilian lands. The war against the indigenous peoples had two truly clear and defined fronts: physical attack on indigenous populations and cultural attack. The physical attack was aimed at the military destruction of the indigenous peoples; the cultural attack aimed at 'integrating' them with colonial ideology and society. These characteristics marked the beginning of the colonization process and are the main characteristics that, for five centuries, governed the relations between the white people and the indigenous peoples, between 'civilized' and 'savage'.

ne of the first actions of the colonizer towards the indigenous peoples was the attempt to enslave them. By the year 1511, about thirty captive indigenous persons had been taken to Lisbon. The Captain-Generals and Donataries of the hereditary captaincies received, by means of Donatary Letters and Charters, the rights to enslave indigenous peoples. The captains had the right to enslave as many indigenous peoples as they wanted and they could take up to thirty-nine to the capital of the colony. The colonizer wished to secure a cheap and abundant supply of labour, but without having to buy black slaves on the African market.

The official and legal beginning of indigenous captivity, however, took place in the year 1537, when a Royal Charter was issued that allowed for the enslavement of the Caetes. During the colonial period

[30] MARTINS JR., Izidoro. **História do Direito Nacional**, Brasília: Ministério da Justiça, 1979. p. 133.

numerous laws and other legal documents were made with the purpose of dealing with the 'freedom' of indigenous peoples. That was the euphemism used to establish the conditions under which the enslavement of indigenous peoples was allowed. Despite the alleged Christian and Catholic faith of the Portuguese Crown, the Court never gave much importance to the commandments of the Church in relation to the delicate problem of indigenous enslavement. It was equally true that the ecclesiastic conception of indigenous enslavement was vacillating and contradictory for a long time. It is notable that in the year 1537, that is, in the same year that the enslavement of the Caetes was permitted, Pope Paul III issued a Bull that excommunicated all those who kept indigenous peoples in captivity.

Legislation on indigenous rights, duties, and enslavement has always been very confusing, despite having a common centre of at least submitting the indigenous peoples to the Catholic religion. So much so that the Statute of Tomé de Souza stated that the main objective of having settlements in Brazil was to bring the 'gentiles into the Catholic faith'. Bringing the gentile into the Catholic faith evidently meant to impose Catholic religion on the indigenous peoples. With the law of 30 July 1609, the indigenous peoples were declared free according to the Law and their natural birth right. The enforcement of this new legislation restored their rights to freedom. Such freedom, however, did not last long, because the law of 10 September 1611 re-established the regime of indigenous enslavement. By this law captivity is deemed legitimate, not only for those captured in just war, but also for those who are rescued from captivity by other indigenous peoples. It was only in 1647 that the law of 13 October 1611 was revoked, which had established conditions for the 'freedom of the gentiles'. In effect, the Charters of 10 November 1647 and 5 and 29 September 1649 restored the regime of freedom of native peoples. It is remarkable though, that following the provision of 17 October 1653, especially designed for the captaincies of Pará and Maranhão, old cases of captivity were restored and new ones were instituted, whereas those of 9 April 1655 abolished the new cases of slavery.

Nevertheless, the incoherence and indecision of the legislation resulted in laws in 1663, 1667, and 1673, that again allowed for the hypothesis of indigenous enslavement. Indigenous enslavement was abolished by the law of 1 April 1680, which reinstated the 30 July 1609 law. In 1684, the law of 2 September once again re-established indigenous enslavement. For the great expert in slavery in Brazil, Perdigão Malheiro, the 2 September law was nothing more than 'disguised slavery'. The definite revocation of indigenous slavery in Brazil only came with the Royal Charter of 27 October 1831.

J. F. Lisboa, quoted by Izidoro Martins Jr.,[31] made a very good synthesis of all the ambiguities and contradictions that marked the enslavement of indigenous peoples:

> Regarding the indians, Portuguese domination was a never interrupted series of hesitations and contradictions up until the ministry of the Marquis of Pombal. One day they decreed unrestrained captivity, the next day absolute freedom, then something in between both extremes. They promulgated, revoked, compromised, according to their will and to current interests and, and finally when they thought the ideas were consolidated once and for all, they started the never-ending thread all over again with new vigour. It was that energetic powerful minister who broke, with no return, the dreadful principle of slavery. Certainly, even after the famous laws of 1755, the indians were often victims of oppression; but in those cases evil had a transitory and merely accidental character, never again acquiring the status of effective doctrine, which, by legitimizing its results, made them even more intense and lasting. The experiments which the government of the Prince Regent attempted in the opposite direction in 1808 were not even well accepted by public opinion, nor able to flourish against the already rooted principle of freedom... A curious specimen of this haphazard and vacillating legislation is the provision of 9 March 1718 that only sums up in a few lines how everything was scattered in dispersed pages for over two centuries... It's easy to imagine all sorts of advantages that eager cruel executors could take from such

[31] MARTINS Junior., Izidoro. **História do Direito Nacional**, Brasília: Ministério da Justiça, 1979. p. 135-136.

> contradictory confusing laws, which by multiplying the cases and the exceptions, gave powerful stimulation to ruse and discretion... Once reduced to captivity, indians and Africans were in all and by all equal in condition and misery. The Portuguese laws, that frequently equated them to beasts and animals and considered them to be things rather than people, consequently treated them in a manner without any sentiment of humanity. The slaves were called pieces. As living and quite perishable breaths, they were cautious of the danger of their loss. As cattle or merchandise, they were marked and stamped so they would not be mistaken for another to the detriment of their respective owners. If they committed crimes, one of the most severe was trying to escape captivity, the owners judged them out loud, without judicial norm or form, and mutilation and hot iron branding, that were already instruments of a good merchant organization and distinctive signs of property, came to rank among the dispositions of political and royal justice... Neither their crude and simple celebrations, nor the ornaments of their women escaped the implacable regulation of the Court!... The exploitation of these miserable pieces was never confined to the limits of slavery, which anyway are so easy to trespass and are always so little respected by the unstoppable greed of the exploiters. As for remorse or the hypocrisy of the Court that was forced to decree the principle of freedom, they kept the resource of ruined free indians to provide idle settlers with working arms... With sweat on their faces and the strength of their arms, they built churches, convents, hospitals, palaces, fortresses, and royal warehouses. They opened roads, farmed lands, harvested the fruits, worked the sugar mills, sailed the canoes, went fishing and hunting, roped cattle, and helped butchers in the butcheries. Finally, the indians fought the offensive and defensive wars in the interests of their oppressors and went along with them on expeditions to the hinterlands to kill, captivate, and take down other indians in their turn.

Izidoro Martins Jr[32] summarized the meaning of Portuguese legislation on the enslavement of the indigenous peoples very well: "Here lies, in its most simple labyrinthine, chaotic, administrative

[32] MARTINS Junior, Izidoro. **História do Direito Nacional**, Brasília: Ministério da Justiça, 1979. p. 139

Proteus features, the extravagant Portuguese legislation on indians in the Brazilian colony."

1.2 Constitutional Rules

The Donatary Letters and the Charters expedited by the Kings of Portugal in favour of the donees of the Hereditary Captaincies and the General Regulations were the first legal texts in effect in Brazil and, in due proportion, they can be considered as the primitive Constitutions of Brazil. The Brazilian Constitution of 1824 did not dedicate any of its items to dealing with indigenous problems. It was absolutely left out. It is curious that the Constitutional Assembly did debate indigenous issues. The results of the debates, however, were classified by Manuela Carneiro da Cunha as "disappointing".[33]

The Constitution of 1891 did not dedicate itself to indigenous matters, even though the debate on aboriginals was present in the Constitutional Assembly. The Positivist Church, in their constitutional proposal, included a text in which they wholly recognized indigenous peoples and their originary rights, thus organizing a confederate model with two models of states with recognized autonomy: (i) the Brazilian Western States that were systematically confederated and originate from the fusion of European, American, and African elements, and (ii) the Brazilian American States, empirically confederated and made up by the "fetishist hordes" spread across the republic.

The first Brazilian Constitution to determine the legal status of the indigenous peoples was the one from 1934, that dedicated two topics on the matter. The 1934 Constitution was based on an assimilationist postulate, seeking to incorporate the "forest dwellers in the national communion" (article 5, section XIX). However, we find the most relevant point in article 129, which established that "the possession of lands of forest dwellers who are permanently located there will be

[33] CUNHA, Manuela Carneiro da. **Os Direitos do Índio**, São Paulo: Brasiliense, 1987. p. 65.

respected, though it may not be disposed of." Commenting on the article, Pontes de Miranda[34] stated that

> "... it respects the 'possession' of the forest dweller, which still requires permanent localization... If there is possession and permanent localization, the land belongs to the native because the Constitution says so, and any transferral of ownership of lands by the forest dwellers, or in lands where they are permanently located and have possession, we highlight, is null."

The 1937 Constitution (article 154) kept similar dispositions to the 1934 one. The liberal regime of 1946 persisted in the perspective of assimilating the indigenous peoples to the "national communion." In the same way, article 216 kept the provisions concerning indigenous lands with similar content to what was previously mentioned. As for the interpretation of article 216 in the 1946 Constitution, the Supreme Federal Court examined the issue in depth in Extraordinary Appeal nº 44.485:

> "This isn't about the common right to property; what has been reserved is the territory of the indigenous peoples. This area was turned into an indigenous park under the custody and administration of the Indian Protection Service, for the lands are not available to them. The goal of the Federal Constitution is that the cultural features of the ancient inhabitants shall remain there, not only for the survival of that tribe but also for studies by ethnologists and studies of other cultural or intellectual nature. It is not really about a concept of ownership or possession in the civil sense of the word; it is about the habitat of a people. *If the Indians, on the date of the Federal Constitution, occupied a certain territory because they got their food resources from there, despite not having constructions or permanent buildings that attest to possession according to our conception, this area, in which and from which they live, was necessary to their subsistence. This area, existing at the time of the Federal Constitution, is what is ordered to be respected.* If it was later reduced by another law; if the State decreased it by ten thousand hectares and tomorrow

[34] Pontes de Miranda. **Comentários à Constituição da República dos E.U. do Brasil.** Rio de Janeiro: Editora Guanabara Waissmann, Koogan, Ltda. Tome II. p. 348.

reduces it by another ten, and ten more later, it could end up confining the Indians to a small space, down to the area of a village, because there 'possession' would be materialized by the huts."

In his exegesis of the constitutional article, Pontes de Miranda[35] argued that:

> "The text respects the 'possession' of the forest dweller, a possession that still requires the assumption of a permanent location. A judge who gets to know about any land issue must apply article 216 given that the prerequisites must be proved by the forest dwellers or appear in the case records, even if some of the parties or a third shows a property title. Once there is possession and permanent location, the land belongs to the native, because the Constitution says so, and any alienation of lands by the forest dwellers or those who are permanently located and with possession, is null, for it infringes the Constitution. The lands that by virtue of article 216 are recognized as being in possession of such peoples, cannot be alienated. Judges cannot issue warrants against forest dwellers who claim possession and are located in those lands permanently. The consequences of the prohibition of alienation are: a) the annulment of any act of provision including those that refer only to elements of the right to ownership or possession (usufruct, real guarantee, tenancy); b) there is no usucapion against forest dwellers even after thirty years; c) sentences that award such lands to another are subject to rescission within the debarment time limit, for violating a constitutional text."

The civic-military regime, implemented in 1964, established through the Constitution of 1967 that the "lands occupied by forest dwellers" were property of the Union (article 4, IV), remaining faithful to the concept of incorporation of indigenous peoples into the national community. However, article 186 of the Constitution of 1967 was more specific regarding the enjoyment of indigenous rights over the lands they occupied. Therefore, the forest dwellers were assured the permanent possession of the lands they inhabit, and their right to the exclusive use of natural resources and all utilities that exist there was recognized."

[35] Pontes de Miranda - **Comentários à Constituição de 1946**, vol. V, 1953. pp. 335-336.

Constitutional Amendment no. 1 of 17 October 1969 persisted in the conception of assimilation of indigenous peoples by the surrounding society (art. 8º, XVII, point o), but it introduced in Paragraph 1 of article 198 that all legal effects, of any nature, of acts having as their object the control, possession, or occupation of lands occupied by forest dwellers, are declared null and void; this nullity was crowned with the prohibition of any compensation. Until 1988, the most remarkable characteristic of the policies and laws concerning indigenous peoples was the constant attempt to integrate them into the so-called national community and thereby making them lose their status as indigenous peoples, turning them into generic Brazilians. The existing differences between indigenous peoples and the 'national community' have always been seen as something to be eliminated through the progressive transformation of indigenous into 'white', that is, insofar as the indigenous peoples give up their cultural difference and assume total identification with the surrounding society.

The Federal Constitution of 1988, when it comes to indigenous peoples, is built upon the very diverse bases that made up the previous Constitutions. First, we must register the great variety of articles dedicated to indigenous peoples (Art. 20, XI; Art. 22, XIV; Art. 109, XI; Art. 129, V; Art. 210, § 2º; Art. 215, § 1º; Art. 231, Art. 232 and 67 of the ADCT [Ato das Disposições Constitucionais Transitórias - Temporary Constitutional Provisions Act]). Here it should be pointed out that for the first time traditional populations were also remembered by the Federal Constitution, which, for example, protected the remaining *quilombo* populations (Art. 216, § 5º and ADCT Art. 68) [*quilombo*: a settlement originally founded by escaped slaves]. As for indigenous lands, the concept of permanently occupied lands (with a permanent character) was abandoned and the concept of lands traditionally occupied by indigenous peoples was adopted. Traditional occupation is not necessarily an immemorial occupation but rather an occupation compatible with the indigenous communities' own way of life. From an economic point of view, we could speak of an occupation outside the mechanisms of the market economy, in the exact constitutional terms: "those [lands] inhabited by them [indians] permanently, they are the lands used for their productive activities, those indispensable for the preservation of the environmental resources necessary for their well-being, and those necessary for their physical and cultural reproduction, according to their usage, customs, and traditions."

Although indigenous lands belong to the Union, they are bestowed permanent enjoyment by indigenous peoples. It is the responsibility of the National Congress to install the authorization, exploitation, and usage of hydraulic and mineral resources in them, "while listening to the affected communities, ensuring their participation in the outcomes of the production, in accordance with the law."

A fundamental constitutional change regarding indigenous lands was the recognition of originary rights over indigenous lands. Originary rights are those that derive from a historical fact, thus recognizing that indigenous peoples were the first occupiers of the national territory, and are not deriving from their fragile and unprotected situation. They attend to rights that pre-exist colonization. It is a similar conception to the one adopted in the Mabo Case, ruled by the Australian Supreme Court.

It is relevant to note that the 1988 Federal Constitution broke with the assimilationist tradition, fully recognizing the cultural peculiarities of the indigenous peoples and establishing legal mechanisms to protect them.

2 Indigenous peoples lands

This topic will present a panoramic view on the concept of 'lands' in the context of Convention 169, as well as in Brazilian Law. As we will see, both concepts are totally compatible.

2.1 Indigenous and Tribal Lands in Convention 169 of the International Labour Organization

Convention 169 adopts a broad definition of the word 'lands', it stipulates in articles 15 and 16 that, following article 13 (1), the term 'lands' shall "include the concept of territories, which encompasses the entire habitat of the regions those peoples occupy or otherwise utilize". This means that such a concept includes places that are not used directly for habitation by indigenous peoples and traditional populations, but serve for carrying out constant essential activities for the physical and cultural reproduction of such human groups, such as hunting grounds or places for religious and cultural practice.

Signatory Countries of Convention 169[36]

Argentina	Guatemala
Plurinational State of Bolivia	Honduras
Brazil	Mexico
Chile	Nepal
Colombia	Nicaragua
Costa Rica	Norway
Dinamarca	the Netherlands
Dominica	Paraguay
Ecuador	Peru
Spain	Bolivarian Republic of Venezuela
Fiji	Central African Republic

[36] GALVIS, Maria Clara and RAMIREZ, Angela. **Manual para defender os direitos dos povos indígenas** (tradução Rodolfo Marinho), Washington: Washington, Due Process of Law Foundation, undated, p. 3.

Convention 169 gives indigenous and tribal peoples the right to property and possession [individual or collective] over lands and territories which they have traditionally occupied. It states that what must be adopted are "measures to safeguard the rights of the people interested in using lands that are not exclusively occupied by them but that they have traditionally had access to for their traditional activities and subsistence" [article 14 (1)]. Still, in such a context, measures must be taken to ensure the protection of their property and possession, with adequate legal mechanisms.

Concerning the natural resources existing in lands and territories traditionally occupied by indigenous and tribal peoples, Convention 169, article 15 (1) determines that they are to be "especially safeguarded", and they certainly include the rights of "these peoples to participate in the use, management and conservation of these resources." Regarding countries that hold the ownership of "mineral or sub-surface resources or rights to other resources pertaining to lands", the States must define procedures that guarantee consultation of the peoples concerned "in order to determine if the interests of these peoples would be harmed, and to what extent, before undertaking or authorizing any programme for prospecting or exploiting the resources present in their lands". Article 15 also establishes that the peoples concerned "must, wherever possible participate in the benefits of such activities, and shall receive fair compensation for any damages which they may sustain as a result of such activities."

An important norm is stipulated in article 16, which defines a general rule of irremovability of indigenous peoples, with some explicit 'reservations' so that evidently there shall not be transference or relocation of these peoples unless considered necessary, article 16 (2), it can only take place with the *consent* of the peoples concerned, "such relocation shall take place only with their free and informed consent". In such a case, it is no longer a mere consultation, but rather an authorization, permission granted by the indigenous and tribal peoples for their relocation to other areas. There is a caveat in Convention 169 that states "Where their consent cannot be obtained, such relocation shall take place only following appropriate procedures established by national laws and regulations, including public inquiries where appropriate, which provide the opportunity for effective representation of the peoples concerned." Once the transfer has been completed and when it is no longer necessary, article 16 (3), "Whenever possible, these peoples shall have the right to return to their traditional lands, as soon as the grounds for relocation cease to exist."

In the event that the return of the indigenous and tribal peoples to their originary lands is not possible, they shall receive – as determined by an agreement or some other appropriate means – new lands whose quality and legal status are "at least equal to the lands previously occupied, allowing them to meet their needs and ensure their future development". If the shifted populations prefer to receive a compensation, "such compensation must be granted with the proper guarantees."

One of the main reasons for the existence of Convention 169 is the defense of the territories of indigenous peoples and traditional populations. Certainly, lands and territories deserve special attention in the Convention. It is important to observe that article 13 (2) establishes the interpretative amplitude that must be imparted to the concept of land and territory, "[t]he use of the term *lands* in Articles 15 and 16 shall include the concept of territories, which covers the total environment of the areas which the peoples concerned occupy or otherwise use."

2.2 Indigenous Lands in Brazilian Law

Since colonial times, Brazilian law has known regulations aimed at indigenous peoples and has always dealt with the issue of lands occupied by the indigenous peoples in a very emphatic way. The theme started to become more and more relevant as the pressure to incorporate indigenous territories into the national economy increased. As noted by Alcida Ramos[37], land is not only a natural resource, it is also a socio-cultural resource of equivalent value. Colonial legislation was full of norms that regulated access and use of indigenous lands, the most

[37] RAMOS, Alcida Rita. **Sociedades Indígenas**, São Paulo: Ática, 1986. Passim.

relevant being the Indian Directory. Rita Heloisa de Almeida[38] understands that "situated in its own time and space, the *Directory* worked as a guide with a breadth equivalent to the Constitutions that rule the nations today".

The concept of frontier, in general, has no great meaning for indigenous peoples. There is a certain tolerance of it, so that groups with different rules can use the same territory. Established limitations are based on a peculiar ethic among the aboriginals. The concepts of house or even village are not of great importance to indigenous peoples. The main element is their territory, their world. It is within this universe that they develop their principal relations. It is unlikely that the society manages to survive and prosper outside of it.

Right at the start of the seventeenth century it was possible to verify that colonial legislation recognized the existence of indigenous lands, that is, of exclusively indigenous lands and dominions. Manuela Carneiro da Cunha[39] informs us that the Royal Charters of 30 July 1609, as well as of 10 September 1611, that were expedited by Philip III, recognized the indigenous peoples' total dominance of their territory and over the lands where their villages are located. Still in the seventeenth century, other licences and governmental acts emerged that provided for indigenous peoples' rights to their lands. This type of legislation inarguably assumed that the Brazilian lands did not belong to the indigenous peoples and that, on the contrary, there should be specific areas within the national territory reserved for them; they also recognized the existence of belligerence among diverse nations.

In this regard, it is interesting to highlight the very wording of the Provision of 1 April 1680, which officially recognized that the indigenous peoples were the first occupants and natural owners of these lands. Due to such recognition, the state started to establish exclusive areas for the indigenous peoples, seeking to compensate for the huge losses they suffered and keep the expansion of colonization under a

[38] ALMEIDA, Rita Heloisa de. **O Diretório dos Índios – Um projeto de "Civilização" no Brasil do Século XVIII**. Brasília: Editora da Universidade de Brasília, 1997. p. 14.
[39] CUNHA, Manuela Carneiro da**. Os Direitos do Índio**, São Paulo: Brasiliense, 1987. p. 58.

certain degree of control. The principal of these compensations is the indication and the recognition of areas that are to be dedicated to the exclusive possession of indigenous peoples.

The Provision of 1 April 1680 was intended to deal with the issues related to the catechesis and the organizing of the indigenous peoples of Maranhão into villages, but in spite of this, it can be presented as a milestone for the legislation dedicated to indigenist problems in general, because according to the License of 8 May 1758, the extension of the determinations until then examined for all indigenous peoples of Brazil was determined. Paragraph 4 of the 1680 License determined that lands should be destined to indigenous peoples descending from the hinterlands. There was the explicit prohibition against relocating forest dwellers from the lands determined to them without their *consent*. Indigenous peoples were not obliged to pay any taxes for their lands.

It is evident that the distance between the legal norm and its concrete application has always been big in our country. We can imagine how much the mentioned rules were disregarded. The fact is that the colonial legislation recognized the indigenous peoples with the exclusive rights to the lands necessary for their survival. Note that the Royal Charter of 9 March 1718 recognized that indigenous peoples "are free and exempt from my jurisdiction, which cannot force them to leave their lands to acquire modes of living not to their liking." It is important to observe that, if a legal prohibition was established, it was evidently because the forbidden situation did indeed take place. If it did not, there would be no need for such a prohibition.

The 'just war' against the indigenous peoples allowed for the subtraction of their lands, turning them into *devolutas* [vacant land]. However, the normative conception of vacant land was only definitively established by Law n. 601 of 18 September 1850. Vacant were those lands given to allottees, whose clauses had been breached, so they returned to the domain of public authority.

The set of legal rules that regulated indigenous lands constitutes the legal framework of the politics of support and protection of indigenous peoples and their culture, known as *indigenato*, which is the primary source of the law and not to be confused with mere possession. This legal institute goes beyond the limits of civil law. It's not common law, but a specialized law. It is particularly relevant to note that the *indigenato* was expressly recognized by the Supreme Federal Court in the trial of the Originary Civil Action 312:[40]

> 25 - Indigenous possession of the land, founded on *indigenato*, is expressed in the ius possessionis and the ius possidendi. It covers the subject's material relation to the thing and the rights of its owners to own it as their habitat.
>
> 26. Accordingly, this Court has decided, with the Constitution of 1946, as voted by Minister VICTOR NUNES LEAL, in RE n. 44.585 [DJ of 11.10. 1961]:
>
> "The goal of the Federal Constitution is that the cultural features of the ancient inhabitants shall remain there, not only for the survival of that tribe but also for studies by ethnologists and studies of other cultural or intellectual nature. It is not really about a concept of ownership or possession, in the civil sense of the forest dwellers; it is about the habitat of a people".
>
> 53 . In the vote I cast in the 'Raposa-Serra do Sol case' (PET n. .388, Rel. Min. Carlos Britto, DJe 24.9.2009), I noted that, even though Brazilian Constitutions only specifically address the issue of indigenous rights in 1934, the matter was a subject of legislation even before the formation of the Brazilian state, as demonstrated in the productive lesson of João Mendes Júnior in his celebrated work "*Os indígenas do Brazil, seus direitos individuais e políticos*" ["The indigenous peoples of Brazil, their individual and political rights"] (São Paulo: Typ. Hennies, Irmãos, 1912), that refers to the License of 1 April 1680, the origin of the *indigenato*, which distinguishes the possession of the indigenous peoples over their lands from the possession of occupation.
>
> In that study, the São Paulo-born author highlighted the situation portrayed in those case files, which cannot be disconsidered even almost one hundred years after his proclamation, *verbis*:

40 http://redir.stf.jus.br/paginadorpub/paginador.jsp?docTP=AC&docID=629999. Accessed on 10/11/2017.

> "The poor indians had no consuls who would intervene for them, they had no judges who recognized their rights to work: they made justice for themselves, as much as it wasn't lawful to expect, because they limited themselves to evasion and dispersion. Some ran away; because, despite all slander, when we want to cut down forests and do heavier works we do not resort to the compatriots of our European grandfathers, but to the descendents of our Indians, to our *caboclos* [people with any degree of indigenous descent], our *caipiras* [humble countryside dweller]." (op. cit., p. 54).
>
> Without judicial bodies to guarantee what colonial law, and then imperial law, assured them, the Indians witnessed the withering of their rights, of their spaces of existence, and of the maintenance of their identities. A situation that not even the advent of the Republic had the capacity to solve, as in the case under evidence of examination, nor subsequent cases.

In the nineteenth century there was a major setback in indigenist law, largely due to the Additional Act of 1834, which conferred competence on the Provincial Assemblies to legislate concurrently with the General Government and the National Assembly on indigenous matters. This resulted in greater power for the oligarchies that were greatly interested in occupying indigenous lands that had always been better protected when they were submitted to central government legislation.

In the Republican period, up until the advent of the 1988 Constitution, the most relevant legislative document is the Indian Statute,[41] which as expected contains a list of articles uniquely directed to dealing with issues related to indigenous lands. In any part of the national territory, the Union can demarcate and allocate areas for the exclusive use of indigenous peoples. Such areas can be acquired by means of purchase, expropriation, or by any other means of transferring ownership.

a) *indigenous reservation:* area destined to serve as habitat for an indigenous group, with sufficient means for their subsistence;

[41] Law no. 6001, of 19 December 1973.

b) *indigenous park:* area within in a land of indigenous possession, whose degree of integration allows for economic, educational, and sanitary assistance by the organs of the Union, and in which reservations of flora, fauna and natural beauty in the region are preserved;

c) *indigenous agricultural colony:* area intended for agriculture and livestock exploitation, administered by the indigenous assistance agency, where acculturated tribes and members of the national community live together;

d) *indigenous federal territory:* is the administrative unit subordinate to the Union, instituted in a region where at least a third of the population is indigenous.

2.2.1 Indigenous Lands in the 1988 Constitution

The importance of the matter is of such magnitude that the Federal Constitution dedicated several articles and sections to it, including those devoted to the social and economic order, which demands a specific law for the development of mining activity in indigenous lands. In the hypothesis of elaborating such a norm, it is necessary to hold a prior Consultation with the indigenous groups. The relevance of the matter is extraordinarily large and the very act of transitional constitutional provisions established a deadline for the demarcation of all indigenous lands. By force of Article 67 of the ADCT [*Ato das Disposições Constitucionais Transitórias* - Temporary Constitutional Provisions Act], the demarcation should be completed within five years time, starting from the promulgation of the Federal Constitution. Such a rule remains in the field of aspiration.

Indigenous peoples were granted originary rights over the land they traditionally occupy, whose concept is as follows: (i) they are the lands used for productive activities; indispensable for the preservation of the necessary environmental resources necessary for their well-being and those necessary for their physical and cultural reproduction, according to their usage, customs, and traditions (art. 231, § 1º); (ii) they are destined for the permanent possession of the indigenous peoples, those responsible for the exclusive use of the riches of the soil, rivers and lakes in them (art. 231, § 2º). The lands traditionally occupied by indigenous peoples, therefore, are not to be mistaken for the lands that were occupied by indigenous peoples since 'time immemorial'. They may or may not be in this condition. The bottom line of this concept is that the lands are essential to the indigenous way of life, nothing else. The temporality of the concept is not considered. However, as we will see, the definition of a time frame for occupation has extraordinary practical consequences.

Indigenous lands are federal public lands and belong to the exclusive domain of the Union. However, the Union itself suffered a limitation of its proprietary rights, since the constituent instituted an exclusive usufruct of the indigenous peoples on the riches of soil, rivers, and lakes in them. Moreover, it determined the inalienability and unavailability of indigenous lands, and their imprescriptible rights over them.

What marks the indigenous lands is that they are indisposable and their rights are not subject to limitation, which is in opposition to the Union and to the indigenous communities themselves, for they cannot undertake any legal business that implies any type of disposition or alienation of their rights over the lands.

The importance of indigenous lands to different indigenous peoples is so great that the Fundamental Law established an indigenous immovability. The indigenous peoples, in the condition of peoples, were constitutionally linked to their turf. The temporary removal of an indigenous people from their land can only happen in cases of an epidemic or catastrophe that puts the very survival of the indigenous population at risk. In the event of the aforementioned hypothesis, the removal must be endorsed by the National Congress. It is also admissible, upon deliberation of the National Congress, that indigenous peoples are removed from their lands when national sovereignty is at risk. Once the risks cease, immediate relocation of the indigenous peoples to their lands of origin must take place.

The Constitution itself determines the absolute nullity and extinction of any legal act that has as its object the occupation, dominion, and possession over indigenous lands. Equally null and void are any acts that have as their object the exploitation of natural riches of soil, rivers, and lakes within indigenous lands. However, there is a caveat for matters of public interest of the Union, as defined by complementary law. The nullities treated in Paragraph 6º of Article 231 do not result in any compensation, except for improvements carried out in good faith.

It will be demonstrated that the Constitutional text is perfectly compatible with the modern humanistic international law of protection of the rights of indigenous and tribal peoples, as defined in Convention 169, in the American Declaration on the Rights of Indigenous Peoples[42] and in the United Nations Declaration on the Rights of Indigenous Peoples.[43]

[42] _http://www.oas.org/es/sadye/documentos/res-2888-16-es.pdf. Accessed on 10/11/2017.
[43] http://www.un.org/esa/socdev/unpfii/documents/DRIPS_pt.pdf. Accessed on 10/11/2017.

CHAPTER 2

Consultation and free, prior and informed consent

Introduction

Free, Prior and Informed Consent is a concept that has been rapidly expanding and can currently be found in different international documents,[44] such as (i) Convention 169 of the International Labour Organization, (ii) the Convention on Biological Diversity, (iii) the Rotterdam Convention on the Prior Informed Consent Procedure for Certain Hazardous Chemicals and Pesticides in International Trade, (v) the Cartagena Protocol, and (vi) the Nagoya Protocol, which are of binding force to the signatories. In addition to the obligatory international documents, there are many international declarations that recognize Free, Prior and Informed Consent, such as (i) the United Nations Declaration on the Rights of Indigenous Peoples, (ii) and the American Declaration on the Rights of Indigenous Peoples.

1 Convention 169 of the International Labour Organization

After many centuries of conflicts and disputes, it was only in the beginning of the twentieth century that an indigenous delegation

[44] TAMANG, Parshuram. *An Overview of the Principle of Free, Prior and Informed Consent and Indigenous Peoples in International and Domestic Law and Practices*, DEPARTMENT OF ECONOMIC AND SOCIAL AFFAIRS, Division for Social Policy and Development, Secretariat of the Permanent Forum on Indigenous Issues, WORKSHOP ON FREE, PRIOR AND INFORMED CONSENT (New York, 17-19 January 2005).

autonomously presented itself on the international scene. It was constituted by a group of Canadian Iroquois (Six Nations) requesting a hearing before the League of Nations, without success.[45] In this regard it is worth recalling that the League of Nations was instituted after the First World War, and one of its founding principles was the autonomy and self-determination of the peoples. It was especially in the 1960s that indigenous and traditional communities started to appear on the international stage as a political force. This situation was favoured by many factors, remarkably (i) decolonization carried out after the Second World War, (ii) internal conflicts in the decolonized countries, with the predominance of certain ethnic groups over others, (iii) the civil rights movement in the United States with the incorporation of ethnic issues by a middle class with indigenous ancestry. It is important to point out that indigenous movements have often clashed with environmentalism – a movement that emerged around the same period – because indigenous demands are closer to the environmental justice discourse that emerged in the United States in the second part of the twentieth century and differs strongly from the main discourse of the environmental movement[46] According to Acselrad, Mello and Bezerra,[47] environmental law came into being as a result of a 'creative articulation' among social, territorial, and environmental demands and civil rights. In Brazil in the 1970s, indigenous peoples manifested themselves very assertively against a predatory model of Amazon occupation, in the same way that traditional peoples did. Nevertheless, it must be mentioned that in Brazil in the 1970s, there was the movement led by Chico Mendes, which had as one of its main points the compatibility between protection of the environment and respect for the lifestyle of traditional peoples,[48] which cost the rubber tapper leader his life. It should be noted

[45] ANAYA, S. James. **International Human Rights and Indigenous Peoples**, New York: Aspen Publishers, 2009, p. 4.

[46] HANNIGAN, John. **Environmental Sociology**, London and New York: Routledge, 3rd edition. 2014, p. 84.

[47] ACSELRAD, Henri; MELLO, Cecília Campello do Amaral and BEZERRA, Gustavo das Neves. **O que é Justiça Ambiental.** Rio de Janeiro: Garamond, 2009, p. 17.

[48] ANTUNES, Paulo de Bessa. **Direito Ambiental**, São Paulo: Atlas, 19th ed., 2017, p. 55.

that most issues raised by indigenous and traditional peoples were related to the possession and use of natural resources within their territories, as well as to the recognition of their ethnic group and human and cultural respect, because "for a colonized people the most essential value, because the most concrete, is first and foremost the land: the land which will bring them bread and, above all, dignity."[49]

The Charter of the United Nations, with its egalitarian spirit, establishes in Article 55 (a) that one of the principles of cooperation between states is to help attain "higher standards of living, full employment, and conditions of economic and social progress and development"; economic cooperation must equally favour "universal respect for, and observance of, human rights and fundamental freedoms for all without distinction as to race, sex, language, or religion" (art. 55 (c)). In turn, the Universal Declaration of Human Rights establishes that "all human beings are born free and equal in dignity and rights" (Article 1), they can invoke them "without distinction of any kind" (Article 2), and it highlights the rights to "life, liberty and security of person" (Article 3) as well as equality "before the law and are entitled without any discrimination to equal protection of the law"(Article 7). Indigenous peoples and traditional populations came to understand themselves as recipients of those human rights and, since then, have been seeking their implementation by all means available to do so.

1.1 Precedents: ILO Convention 107

The ILO is the oldest international organization in existence today. It was created in 1919 as one of the consequences of the Treaty of Versailles which ended the First World War. One of its most remarkable features is its tripartite constitution, bringing together in its executive bodies representatives of governments, employees and employers.

[49] FANON, Frantz, **The Wretched of the Earth**, preface by Jean-Paul Sartre, translated by Constance Farrington Grove Weidenfeld, New York. 1963, p. 80.

ILO's concern with indigenous populations has a long history, and as early as 1921 the organization began to adopt measures in relation to the 'native workers' that were directed at the situation of workers in colonial countries. In 1930 the ILO approved Convention 29[50] on forced or compulsory labour.[51] Convention 29 focused on the situation of indigenous workers rather than of indigenous peoples. It was only after the Second World War that indigenous and tribal peoples themselves started to get the ILO's attention. This was materialized with a pilot programme targeting the indigenous peoples of the Andes, developed between 1952 and 1972. From the Andean experience, new initiatives were developed, and the UN requested that the ILO moved forward by making an international convention on indigenous peoples. Those initiatives led to the adoption of Convention 107 in 1957. Convention 107 was endorsed by 27 countries, including 14 from the Americas and also by African and Asian countries. However, the Convention reflected the thinking of the time, and was not concerned with the indigenous point of view on their issues and it clearly adopted integrationist and assimilist perspectives that sought to dissolve indigenous peoples in national societies.

Convention 107 was endorsed by Brazil and incorporated into national law by Decree n. 58.824 of 14 July 1966. At this point, it is important to state that it provided for the "Protection and Integration of Indigenous and Other Tribal and Semi-Tribal Populations in Independent Countries". The recitals of the Convention start from the conception that "all human beings have the right to pursue both their material well-being and their spiritual development in conditions of freedom and dignity, of economic security and equal opportunity". Nevertheless,

> "there exist in various independent countries indigenous and other tribal and semi-tribal populations *which are not yet integrated into the national community* and whose social, economic or cultural situation

[50] Ratified by Brazil only on 25 April 1957.

[51] ANAYA, S. James. **International Human Rights and Indigenous Peoples**, New York: Aspen Publishers, 2009, p. 135.

hinders them from benefiting fully from the rights and advantages enjoyed by other elements of the population".

Therefore, it becomes necessary that the international community take measures that are capable of facilitating "action to assure the protection of the populations concerned, their progressive integration into their respective national communities, and the improvement of their living and working conditions". The elaboration of the Convention involved the collaboration of the UN, the Food and Agriculture Organization of the United Nations, the United Nations Organization for Education, Science and Culture, and of the World Health Organization, it was not a work solely produced by the ILO.

In 1986, Convention 107 was under severe criticism by indigenous peoples and began to be revised. For the first time, this included the participation of two non-governmental organizations linked to indigenous rights [Survival International and The World Council of Indigenous Peoples (WCIP)[52]. In the revision process, the most contentious and controversial theme was the replacement of the term 'populations' with 'peoples', although all issues related to indigenous lands also incited heated controversies. According to Dorough's notes,[53] the discussions about lands included topics such as property and possession, protection of property rights, control over natural resources, consent of indigenous peoples to be granted before starting prospecting or mining production works, prohibition of relocating indigenous lands, occupation or non-authorized use of indigenous lands, and rules

[52] DOROUGH, Dalee Sambo. **The Revision of International Labour Organization Convention no. 107: A Subjective Assessment,** in, DUNBAR-ORTIZ, Roxanne; DOROUGH, Dalee Sambo, ALFREDSSON, Gudmundur; SWEPSTON, Lee e WILLE, Petter (Edited by), **Indigenous Peoples' Rights In International Law: Emergence and Application - Book in Honor of Asbjørn Eide at Eighty**. Kautokeino & Kopenhagen: Gáldu & IWGIA, 2015, p. 250.

[53] DOROUGH, Dalee Sambo. **The Revision of International Labour Organization Convention no. 107: a Subjective Assessment,** in, DUNBAR-ORTIZ, Roxanne; DOROUGH, Dalee Sambo, ALFREDSSON, Gudmundur; SWEPSTON, Lee e WILLE, Petter (edited by), **Indigenous Peoples' Rights In InternatIonal Law: Emergence and application - Book in Honor of Asbjørn Eide at Eighty**. Kautokeino & Kopenhagen: Gáldu & IWGIA, 2015, p. 253.

for reclaiming territories. Few delegations were composed of individuals with proven expertise in indigenous matters, however, Portugal, Colombia, and Ecuador were represented by people "with particular expertise in the area of indigenous human rights and who were very knowledgeable and supportive of indigenous concerns."[54]

The Convention is divided into eight parts (general policy; land; recruitment and conditions of employment; vocational training, handicrafts and rural industries; social security and health; education and means of communication; administration; and general provisions) that are subdivided over 37 articles. The revision of Convention 107 led to the adoption of Convention 169, which basically kept the same structure, but with a few very significant conceptual changes.

The subjects in the Convention were radically altered. The concept of "members of tribal or semi-tribal populations" (Convention 107, Article 1 (a)) was abandoned and replaced by the concept of indigenous or tribal 'peoples'. The change was even more profound, because Convention 107 assumed that tribal or semi-tribal populations were "at a less advanced stage than the stage reached by the other sections of the national community". The criteria for identifying indigenous and tribal peoples that came to be adopted according to Articles 1 (1) (a), (b) and (2) of Convention 169, can be broken down into objective aspects (1): (i) tribal peoples whose social, cultural and economic conditions distinguish them from other sections of the national community, and whose status is regulated wholly or partially by their own customs or traditions or by special laws or regulations; (ii) peoples regarded as indigenous on account of their descent from the populations which inhabited the country, or a geographical region to which the country belongs, at the time of conquest or colonisation or the establishment of present state boundaries and who, irrespective of their legal status,

[54] DOROUGH, Dalee Sambo. **The Revision of International Labour Organization Convention no. 107: a Subjective Assessment,** in, DUNBAR-ORTIZ, Roxanne; DOROUGH, Dalee Sambo, ALFREDSSON, Gudmundur; SWEPSTON, Lee e WILLE, Petter (edited by), **Indigenous Peoples' Rights In International Law: Emergence and application - Book in Honor of Asbjørn Eide at Eighty**. Kautokeino & Kopenhagen: Gáldu & IWGIA, 2015, p. 255.

retain some or all of their own social, economic, cultural and political institutions. In addition, there is the subjective aspect (2) provided for in Article 1 (2) which is that the self-identification as indigenous or tribal shall be regarded as a fundamental criterion for determining the groups to which the provisions of Convention 169 apply.

With regard to the criteria for identifying indigenous and tribal peoples, it is worth noting the vote of Minister Rosa Weber in the ADI 3239 [*Ação Direta de Inconstitucionalidade* - Direct Action of Unconstitutionality], still pending before the Supreme Federal Court,[55] in which she stated that:

> "The choice for self-attribution criteria isn't arbitrary, unfounded or unbiased. Besides consisting of a method authorized by contemporary anthropology, it sets out a public policy option that is legitimated by the Republican Charter in a way that it aims to interrupt the process of the systematic denial of the identity of marginalized groups."

It was also added that the self-attribution of an identity (subjective criterion) is not enough to deviate from objective criteria required for the recognition of the entitlement of the rights granted by Article 68 of the ADCT, in relation to the *quilombolas* [runaway slaves];living in *quilombos*].

> "It appears to be necessary to satisfy an objective element: the reproduction of the social unit that is said to originate from a quilombo must be tied to a continued occupation of the still existing space, organically, on 5 October 1988."

Finally, the term indigenous peoples doesn't have the same usual meaning in the context of Convention 169 as it does in international law. The aforementioned alterations marked the shift from an assimilationist and integrationist conception of indigenous and tribal peoples to another that recognizes the cultural autonomy of these populations, recognizing their right to self-determination.

[55] http://www.stf.jus.br/portal/cms/verNoticiaDetalhe.asp?idConteudo=288144. Accessed on 15/10/2017.

1.1.2 Convention 169 of the International Labour Organization

Convention 169 is an 'update' of Convention 107 that, however, has taken on a life of its own for adopting an entirely different concept from that of Convention 107. The examination of all the terms of Convention 169 lies beyond the scope for this work, for this reason we shall only examine those related to *Consultation* (art. 6 (2)) and to *Consent* (art 16 (2)) that should be sought together with indigenous and tribal peoples, related to matters concerning issues of relevant interest to such human communities. Before tackling the subject, it is important to note that Convention 169 is the broadest international treaty on the rights of indigenous and tribal peoples, it deals with the most relevant aspects related to the lives of said populations, and it is certainly one of the most comprehensive international instruments with binding force intended to protect the rights of indigenous and tribal peoples.

The so-called prior informed consent of indigenous and tribal peoples for intervention on their territories is a complex subject, for it involves issues related, for example, to (i) the legitimate authority summoning a consultation; (ii) the juridical nature of the consultation; (iii) applicable modes and procedures; (iv) legitimacy and representation of the participants of the consultation; and many others deserving accurate examination.

1.3 Convention on Biological Diversity

The Convention on Biological Diversity (CBD) was signed in 1992 during the United Nations Conference on Environment and Development, held in Rio de Janeiro; it is one of the key records that ensures the protection of ecosystems and concurrently promotes a long-awaited sustainable development, one that is capable of supplying the needs of the current generation without compromising the ability to attend to the needs of future generations, that is to say, it is a development that doesn't exhaust natural resources in the future.

The CBD was incorporated into Brazilian Law by Decree n. 2.519 of 16 March 1988. The Convention has two very relevant protocols, namely (i) the Cartagena Protocol[56] and (ii) the Nagoya Protocol. Brazil is part only of the first. All three international documents assume Prior Consultation.

Article 8 (j) of the CBD establishes that "each Contracting Party must, as far as possible and as appropriate...", and

> "...subject to its national legislation, respect, preserve and maintain knowledge, innovations and practices of indigenous and local communities embodying traditional lifestyles relevant for the conservation and sustainable use of biological diversity and promote their wider application with the approval and involvement of the holders of such knowledge, innovations and practices and encourage the equitable sharing of the benefits arising from the utilization of such knowledge, innovations and practices".

Also in Articles 15 (4) and (5) it is possible to identify the need for Prior Consultation for the transfer of genetic resources.

The procedural question, that is, the mechanism with which local communities and indigenous populations will or will not consent to the access to associated traditional knowledge is treated in Article 15 (5) of the CBD. It must be *prior* and *substantiated*, unless the state which is party to the Convention, in its internal legislation, has established otherwise. Therefore, it seems clear that the Consultation of local communities and indigenous peoples must be promoted before access and certainly with full explanation of the activities that will be carried out. The same Article 15, in paragraph 7, establishes the obligation that the Contracting Parties take "legislative, administrative or policy measures, as appropriate", in order to establish mechanisms for "sharing

[56] "Protocol is a term that has been employed in many senses, as much in bilateral agreements as in multilateral ones. It seems to designate agreements less formal than treaties, or complementary or interpretative agreements of treaties or previous conventions. It is also used to designate the completed minutes of an international conference. It has often been used in Brazilian diplomatic practice in the form of a "protocol of intent", to mark the beginning of a commitment." (BRASIL, Ministry of Foreign Affairs, apud ANTUNES, 2017, p. 774).

in a fair and equitable way the results of research and development and the benefits arising from the commercial and other utilization of genetic resources with the Contracting Party providing such resources. Such sharing shall be upon mutually agreed terms".

As we have seen, the Convention on Biological Diversity is quite explicit in terms of its distributive nature relating to the benefits acquired from the access to associated traditional knowledge, and it is also very categorical about the fact that the providers of genetic resources and traditional knowledge must be priorly and adequately informed, in order to issue a judicially valid consent.

The Cartagena Protocol, incorporated into Brazilian Law with Decree no. 5.705 of 16 February 2006, is an additional agreement to the Convention on Biological Diversity which aims to ensure the safe handling, transport and use of living modified organisms resulting from modern biotechnology that may have adverse effects on biological diversity. Although it is not directly targeted at indigenous and tribal peoples, the Protocol establishes many consultation and consent mechanisms for the transboundary transportation of living modified organisms.

The so-called Bonn Guidelines on Access to Genetic Resources and Fair and Equitable Sharing of the Benefits Arising out of their Utilization were adopted at COP VI [Conference of the Parties], Decision VI/24.[57] The need for these Guidelines, of course, came from the fact that the CBD provisions are broad and somewhat abstract, requiring a certain concreteness. Furthermore, the lack of Guidelines for the states that were party to CBD to adopt, – or the attempt to adopt similar conceptions on the crucial issues of access to genetic resources, Prior Informed Consent and the transfer of technology – could imply that the Convention on Biological Diversity turns into truly hollow words, or a mere declaration of intentions. This way, the international community gathered at COP VI established the general terms to be followed by the Contracting Parties when they establish policies, norms, and internal procedures related to the aforementioned subjects.

[57] https://www.cbd.int/abs/bonn. Accessed on 14/10/2017.

Naturally, the guidelines are not mandatory for the states, they should adopt them voluntarily.

The Nagoya Protocol is a supplementary agreement to the Convention of Biological Diversity. Its main objective is to regulate the access of indigenous and traditional peoples to the sharing of benefits arising out of the utilization of genetic resources, as established by Article 8 (j) of the CBD. Brazil has not ratified the Nagoya Protocol despite having participated in the negotiations.

The Bonn Guidelines, under item C, seek to define the ways we must concretize Article 15 of the CBD, safeguarding the sovereign rights of the Parties over their natural resources. It should be noted that Paragraph 5 of Article 15 establishes that the access to genetic resources shall be subject to *Prior Informed Consent* of the Contracting Party providing such resources, following logically that, in the context of CBD, the consent of the Party (a member state of the Convention) must necessarily pass through the Prior Informed Consent of local communities and indigenous populations who hold traditional knowledge associated with biological diversity. In view of this, the guidelines established basic principles to be observed by the Contracting Parties when deciding their internal law on the matter.

The basic principles to be observed in the establishment of norms for prior informed consent are:

(a) Legal certainty and clarity;

(b) Access to genetic resources should be facilitated at minimum cost.

(c) Restrictions on access to genetic resources should be transparent, based on legal grounds, and not run counter to the objectives of the CBD;

(d) Consent of the relevant competent national authority in the provider country.

Consent from relevant stakeholders such as local communities and indigenous populations must be obtained when appropriate to the circumstances, according to applicable domestic legislation.

The constitutive elements of informed consent must include the following:

(a) Competent authority granting or providing for evidence of prior informed consent;
(b) Timing and deadlines;
(c) Specification of use;
(d) Procedures for obtaining prior informed consent;
(e) Mechanism for the consultation of relevant stakeholders,
(f) Process.

As for the rights to intellectual property related to the access to traditional knowledge associated with biological diversity, in Brazil this matter is treated in Law no. 13.123/2015. It should be noted that the term traditional knowledge can, in this context, have a wide scope including traditional knowledge of agriculture, biological diversity, medicine, and folklore. It still doesn't have a definition accepted without contestation at the international level.[58] The World Intellectual Property Organization (WIPO) considers that traditional knowledge encompasses the intangible intellectual and cultural heritage of local and indigenous communities, that is, the content of knowledge itself, as well as traditional cultural expressions, including distinctive symbols and signs associated with traditional knowledge. Traditional knowledge can be codified, that is, it can be systematized, organized, and classified by the traditional communities themselves, as is the case with traditional medicine. According to WIPO, the World Health Organization (WHO) distinguishes between (i) coded systems of traditional medicine present in ancient scriptures that are entirely in the public domain, as is the case, for instance, with the Sanskrit scriptures containing Ayurveda or texts of Chinese Traditional Medicine, and (ii) unwritten knowledge that remains in the memory and in practices orally passed down generations.

It is important to note that the use of genetic resources doesn't always derive from associated traditional knowledge and that, in the same way, not all traditional knowledge is related to the use of genetic resources,[59] as explained in the Bonn Guidelines (Decision 24/ COP 6).

[58] http://www.wipo.int/tk/en/resources/glossary.html#49. Accessed on 14/10/2017.
[59] http://www.cbd.int/decision/cop/default.shtml?id=7198. Accessed on 14/10/2017.

Article 2, VI of Law no. 13.123, of 20 May 2015 defines Prior Informed Consent as "formal consent, previously conceded by an indigenous population or traditional community according to their uses, customs, traditions, or communitary protocols." The first aspect that stands out from this definition is that it must be formal, that is, it must be provided in an unequivocal and registrable way. Article 9 establishes that the access to associated traditional knowledge of identifiable origin is under the condition of acquiring Prior Informed Consent. By condition we understand that if there is no Prior Informed Consent, access is illegal. However, Paragraph 1 of the same Article 9 establishes formal mechanisms capable of demonstrating, "at the discretion of the indigenous population, traditional community, or traditional farmer", the prior informed agreement of local communities, indigenous populations, and traditional farmers with specific access to traditional knowledge associated with biological diversity. Thus, it is up to the relevant stakeholders in each case, according to the Bonn Guidelines, to indicate the manner in which they will or will not express prior informed consent.

Nevertheless, it would be reasonable for the Law to establish, even if succinctly, the basic guidelines for carrying out the consultations, thereby minimizing as much as possible the legal uncertainties that will certainly appear in such a complex area, from a legal point of view. They will often appear at the junction of juridical universes that are not always founded on the same rationality, given the historical, social, cultural, religious, and many other differences among diverse human groups. Indeed, out of 4 (four) possibilities for formalization stipulated by the norm, only 1 (one) concerns the procedures of the communities themselves, an accession stipulated by communitary protocol. The other forms are (i) signature of the prior consent agreement; (ii) audiovisual record of the consent; and (iii) a report by the competent official agency.

It is important to notice that the number and diversity of traditional communities have been expanding significantly. In a way, it's about the rebirth of communities that in one way or another were 'invisible' in the eyes of national societies and now claim (i) cultural and ethnic recognition, (ii) economic compensation or other kinds of compensation for the use of their knowledge, and (iii) adequate processes to ensure their participation in relevant decisions about their destinies.

1.4 Other Conventions

1.4.1 Convention on the Control of Transboundary Movements of Hazardous Wastes and their Disposal [Basel Convention]

The Convention was incorporated into Brazilian Law by Decree no. 875, of 19 July 1993. Although it acknowledges reservations about some parts of the Convention Text, it affirms:

> "1. By adhering to the Basel Convention on the Control of Transboundary Movements of Hazardous Wastes and their Disposal, the Brazilian Government associates itself with an instrument it considers to be positive, as it establishes international mechanisms for the control of such movements - based on the principle of *prior and explicit consent* to the import and transit of hazardous wastes –, it aims to curb illicit trafficking and stipulates the intensification of international cooperation for the adequate management of said wastes."

1.4.2 The Rotterdam Convention on the Prior Informed Consent Procedure for Certain Hazardous Chemicals and Pesticides in International Trade – PIC

The Convention was adopted in September 1998 and has been in force since 24 February 2004, when it was ratified by fifty countries. It was incorporated into Brazilian Law by Legislative Decree no. 197, of 7 May 2004, and promulgated by Decree no. 5360, of 31 January 2005. The Convention is not specifically related to the concession of consent or to the consultation of indigenous peoples. The document deals with countries' consent to international commerce of certain chemical substances and dangerous pesticides.

1.4.3 The Stockholm Convention on Persistent Organic Pollutants

The so-called POPs Convention was incorporated into Brazilian Law by Decree no. 5472 of 20 June, 2005, and it determines the need for Prior Informed Consent for matters related to transportation, storagerage, waste waste disposal, and other measures related to organic pollutants. The *consideranda* of the Convention already recall the "pertinent provisions of relevant international environmental conventions, especially the Rotterdam Convention on the Prior Informed Consent Procedure for Certain Hazardous Chemicals and Pesticides in International Trade and the Basel Convention on the Control of Transboundary Movements of Hazardous Wastes and their Disposal, including the regional agreements developed within the framework of its Article 11", which indicates that Prior Consent is definitely incorporated into environmental issues, and evidently is related to human rights, as is the case with indigenous and tribal peoples.

Article 3 (2) (b) determines that each party must adopt measures to guarantee that export, subject to prior informed consent, of certain substances is made according to the following criteria: i) for the purpose of environmentally sound disposal as set forth in paragraph 1 (d) of Article 6; or, ii) To a Party which is permitted to use that chemical under Annex A or Annex B; or, iii) To a State not Party to this Convention which has provided an annual certification to the exporting Party. Such certification shall specify the intended use of the chemical and include a statement that, with respect to that chemical, the importing State is committed to: a. Protect human health and the environment by taking the necessary measures to minimize or prevent releases; b. Comply with the provisions of paragraph 1 of Article 6; and c. Comply, where appropriate, with the provisions of paragraph 2 of Part II of Annex B.

1.5 The United Nations Declaration on the Rights of Indigenous Peoples

On 13 September 2007, the UN adopted the United Nations Declaration on the Rights of Indigenous Peoples, which is known not to be a binding document.[60] The Declaration was adopted by an overwhelming majority of countries during the UN General Assembly, with 144 votes in favour, four against (Canada, New Zealand, Australia and the United States) and eleven abstentions amongst the votes against. The final text was approved after about twenty-five years of negotiations.

The preamble of the Declaration affirms that indigenous peoples are equal to all other peoples, while recognizing the right of all peoples to be different, to consider themselves different, and to be respected as such. The preamble indicates that the control by indigenous peoples over developments affecting them and their lands, territories and resources will enable them to maintain and strengthen their institutions, cultures and traditions, and to promote their development in accordance with their aspirations and needs, recognizing also that respect for indigenous knowledge, cultures and traditional practices contributes to sustainable and equitable development and proper management of the environment.

Free, prior and informed Consent is contained in Article 10, which determines that indigenous peoples shall not be forcibly removed from their lands or territories, and that "no relocation shall take place without the free, prior and informed consent of the indigenous peoples concerned and after agreement on just and fair compensation and, where possible, with the option of return." It is also mentioned in Article 11 (2), which determines that the States shall provide redress "through effective mechanisms, which may include restitution, developed in conjunction with indigenous peoples, with respect to their

[60] https://treaties.un.org/pages/overview.aspx?path=overview/glossary/page1_en.xml#declarations, Accessed on 13/10/2017.

cultural, intellectual, religious and spiritual property taken without their free, prior and informed consent or in violation of their laws, traditions and customs." When it comes to legislative or administrative measures that may affect indigenous peoples, Article 19 stipulates that "States shall consult and cooperate in good faith with the indigenous peoples concerned through their own representative institutions in order to obtain their free, prior and informed consent before adopting and implementing legislative or administrative measures that may affect them."

Moreover, Article 28 (1) stipulates the right of indigenous peoples to redress, by means that can include restitution or, when this is not possible, of a just, fair and equitable compensation, for the lands, territories and resources which they have traditionally owned or otherwise occupied or used, "and which have been confiscated, taken, occupied, used or damaged without their free, prior and *informed* consent.". Finally, Article 29 (2) deals with hazardous wastes and establishes that "States shall take effective measures to ensure that no storage or disposal of hazardous materials shall take place in the lands or territories of indigenous peoples without their free, prior and informed consent."

1.6 The American Declaration on the Rights of Indigenous Peoples

The General Assembly of the Organization of American States approved the American Declaration on the Rights of Indigenous Peoples on 14 June 2006, after years of debates. The Declaration follows the lead taken by Convention 169 and the UN Declaration on the Rights of Indigenous Peoples, by broadly establishing the need for prior Consultation and Consent for a range of issues involving indigenous peoples and their rights.

Article XIII (2) establishes that states shall provide redress through effective mechanisms, which may include restitution, developed in conjunction with indigenous peoples, with respect to their cultural, intellectual, religious, and spiritual property taken without their free, prior, and informed consent or in violation of their laws, traditions, and customs. Concerning the participation of indigenous peoples in matters of their interest, the Declaration claims in Article XXIII (2) that states shall consult and cooperate in good faith with the indigenous peoples concerned, through their own representative institutions, in order to obtain their free, prior and informed consent *before* adopting and implementing legislative or administrative measures that may affect them.

Finally, on the issue of protection of cultural heritage and intellectual property, Article XXVIII (3) establishes that the states, with the full and effective participation of indigenous peoples, shall adopt measures necessary to ensure that national and international agreements and regimes provide recognition and adequate protection for the cultural heritage of indigenous peoples and intellectual property associated with that heritage.

CHAPTER 3

Financial institutions and indigenous and tribal peoples

Introduction

The different international Treaties, Conventions, and Declarations examined above have generated and still generate repercussions on international agencies for economic development that are part of the United Nations system.

Likewise, they generate repercussions on private institutions, by bringing the so-called 'indigenous issue' to the centre of the economical debate, when it comes to financing extractivist activities to be carried out (or that have influence) over indigenous or tribal territories. Moreover, since the end of the last century indigenous and tribal peoples have strongly resisted the use of their territory without their prior authorization to do so, or even when they were properly compensated by the negative impacts caused on their lands, their mode of living, culture, and other legally protected assets at an international and local level.

For financial and developmental institutions, on the other hand, the lack of a formal approval by indigenous and tribal peoples of the use of their territories allows for the creation of a series of risks for the funding agents, such as:

(i) instability of projects due to indigenous peoples and traditional populations' disapproval,

(ii) damage to the institutional image,

(iii) international public opinion reproval for violating human rights.

These and other concerns caused the international financial system to start looking at the execution conditions of the big infrastructure projects they finance, demanding a care that was previously unimaginable. As we know, the international financial system was set up in the last days of the Second World War and in the immediate post-war period. When the conflict had ended, the UN, founded in San Francisco in 1945, instituted the World Bank,[61] which has been through many transformations since its creation and today is a conglomerate involving different institutions that "evolved from the International Bank for Reconstruction and Development (IBRD) as a facilitator of post-war development and reconstruction, up to the current mandate of poverty reduction." As development promoter, the World Bank has an important role in financing large governmental projects. The International Finance Corporation is an institution basically focused on financing large projects developed by the private sector. The Inter-American Development Bank[62] was instituted in the Americas, and its goals are very close to those of the World Bank. A process of very severe criticism against the loans granted by the Development Banks has been growing since the 1970s, because according to critics, those loans were contributing to the implementation of projects that were socially and environmentally disastrous, causing extremely grave consequences for the populations affected by the enterprises. It is notable that one of the first waves of international protest was started by the loans for the so-called Polonoroeste project in the Brazilian Amazon region.[63]

Another relevant multilateral institution that emerged at the end of the Second World War is the International Monetary Fund (IMF), created by forty-four countries in Bretton Woods in July 1944. Among its basic purposes was building a framework for international economic cooperation capable of avoiding a repetition of "the vicious cycle of

[61] http://www.bancomundial.org/es/about/history. Accessed on 10/06/2017.

[62] http://www.iadb.org/en/inter-american-development-bank,2837.html. Accessed on 12/10/2017.

[63] ANTUNES, Paulo de Bessa. **Direito Ambiental**, São Paulo: Atlas, 19th edition, 2017, p. 724.

competitive currency devaluations that contributed to the Great Depression of the 1930s".[64] Currently, the IMF's primary mission is "to ensure the stability of the international monetary system". The IMF provides technical assistance and training to the 189 member countries promoting "policies designed to foster economic stability, reduce vulnerability to economic and financial crises, and raise living standards."

All these mechanisms express the introduction of the development concept that became ubiquitous after the Second World War. 'Development' became a mission for almost all governments from that moment on it became a mantra recited by all countries, especially the young nations coming out of the process of decolonization, which greatly accelerated at the end of the 1950s. Indigenous and tribal peoples, with their strong critique, unveiled the harmful aspect of development, which until then had only been seen as positive, the negative outcomes it generated were not considered. As Robert Goodland[65] observed, "giving consideration to people affected by development is a relatively new process". According to him, in the 1950s and 1960s there was no possibility that those affected by large projects could have their complaints heard and considered by public authorities. However, in the 1980s the World Bank introduced the concept of 'meaningful consultation' for the projects it financed, and in 1992 stakeholder's participation became mandatory. When it comes to indigenous peoples, it must be noted that economic studies carried out by the IMF demonstrate that indigenous and tribal peoples are listed among the poorest of the poorest in Latin America.[66] They are certainly the ones who suffer the most from the negative aspects of development,

[64] http://www.imf.org/external/np/exr/facts/glance.htm. Accessed on 03/07/2015.

[65] GOODLAND, Robert. "**Free, Prior and Informed Consent and the World Bank Group.**" Sustainable Development Law and Policy, Summer 2004, p. 66.

[66] HALL, Gilbert e PATRINOS, Anthony, **Latin America`s Indigenous Peoples, Finance and Development,** December 2005, Volume 42, Number 4, in, http://www.imf.org/external/pubs/ft/fandd/2005/12/hall.htm#author. Accessed on 03/07/2015.

especially when it comes to the implementation of extractivist industries or the construction of large dams.

1 Polonoroeste project and the World Bank's change of direction

One of the first projects partially financed by the World Bank to be criticized by indigenous and tribal peoples and their support groups, was the Polonoroeste project, implemented in Brazil in the Amazon region in the beginning of the 1980s.

Polonoroeste was created by Decree nº 86.029, 0n 27 May 1981 and encompassed

> "the area of influence of the Cuiabá - Porto Velho road link, covering the west and the northwest of Mato Grosso state (the cities Cuiabá, Várzea Grande, Nossa Senhora do Livramento, Poconé, Cáceres, Mirassol d'Oeste, Barra do Bugres, Tangará da Serra, Vila Bela da Santíssima Trindade, the west part of the Roosevelt river in the city of Aripuanã) and the Federal Territory of Rondônia."

According to a report by Betty Mindlin,[67] the indigenous population in the project area was ten thousand people, members of about 80 indigenous groups, of which "15 were still isolated in the forest". The goals of the project were to: (i) contribute to greater national integration; (ii) promote an adequate demographic occupation of the programme-region, absorbing economically marginalized populations of other regions and providing employment; (iii) reach a significant increase in regional production and in the income of its population; (iv) favour the reduction of development inequality, at inter and intra-regional levels; and (v) guarantee production growth in harmony with concerns about preserving the ecological system and protecting indigenous communities, in accordance with the creation decree. The interventions Polonoroeste intended to make were: (i) the reconstruction and paving of the Cuiabá - Porto Velho highway; (ii) the

[67] MINDLIN, Betty. Índios e grandes projetos econômicos—um exemplo: o programa Polonoroeste (Mato Grosso e Rondônia, 1982-87). São Paulo: Instituto de Antropologia e Meio Ambiente, June 1988, in, http://bd.trabalhoindigenista. org.br/ sites /default/files/CTI02031.pdf. Accessed on 11/11/2017.

construction and consolidation of the local road network; (iii) the implementation and consolidation of integrated colonization and directed settlement projects; (iv) the execution of landholding regularization services; (v) giving support to productive activities (research and agricultural experiments, technical assistance and rural extension, credit, storage, and trading), as well as the expansion of social services (education and health) and infrastructure improvement in small rural communities; and (v) the preservation of the ecological system and support for indigenous communities.

Between 1981 and 1985, the Polonoroeste budget was about "Cr$ 77.308.000.000.00 (seventy seven billion and three hundred and eight million cruzeiros), at the prices of January 1981, excluding rural credit". The World Bank contributed with US$ 346.4 million in financing. According to Phillip Fearnside,[68] most of the budget, about 57% of the US$ 1.55 billion for the project in the 1981-1985 period, was destined for the complete reconstruction and paving of a 1500 km section of the Marechal Rondon highway (BR-364), connecting Cuiabá to Porto Velho. Only 3% of the project's budget was allocated to the protection of indigenous lands and areas of environmental value.

Despite one of its institutional goals being to "guarantee production growth in harmony with concerns about preserving of the ecological system and protecting indigenous communities", the project faced strong resistance from indigenous peoples located in the project's area of influence, especially due to the planned use of their territories without making any form of consultation or agreement with the impacted communities.

The Survival International association, an important support group for indigenous and tribal peoples, indicated in a report published at the time of the occurrence, that between 1984 and 1985 several conflicts took place in the indigenous areas affected by Polonoroeste. The first

[68] FEARNSIDE, P.M. 1987. **Frenesi de Desmatamento no Brasil: A Floresta Amazônica Irá Sobreviver?** pp. 45-57, in: G. Kohlhepp and A. Schrader (eds.) **Homem e Natureza na Amazônia.** Tübinger Geographische Studien 95 (Tübinger Beiträge zur Geographischen Lateinamerika-Forschung 3). Geographisches Institut, Universität Tübingen, Tübingen, Germany. p. 51.

was registered in the indigenous area of Igarapé Lourdes, inhabited by the Gavião, Arara and Zoró peoples, and included the taking of hostages by indigenous people. Many other similar conflicts took place involving other ethnicities.[69] It is a fact that today the echoes of those past mistakes made by the World Bank in the Polonoroeste case are still resounding, which generates severe distrust regarding the procedures adopted by the financial institution.[70] Unfortunately, there are several other cases that indicate the existence of financing that ended up resulting in controversial interventions with negative impacts on the environment and on traditional communities and indigenous peoples. The World Bank recognizes that its relations with indigenous peoples have often been tense and marked by a lack of trust.[71]

The facts described above gradually led the World Bank to start using environmental and social criteria for granting financing to projects with an impact on traditional populations.

1.1 World Bank Policies

According to Shelton Davis[72] the World Bank's first directive related to indigenous peoples was OMS 2.34, issued in February 1982. However, the Bank had already started studies related to the subject, from the perspective of the ILO Convention 107, that is, with an integrationist conception of indigenous peoples towards the development process. According to Davis, the publication of the World

[69] Cultural Survival, Quarterly, 10.2 (Summer 1986), Land Rights: Strategies for Survival, in http://www.culturalsurvival.org/publications/cultural-survival-quarterly/brazil/warfa re-polonoroeste. Accessed on 10/06/2017.

[70] CARVALHO, Guilherme. Os Bancos Multilaterais e o Complexo Rio Madeira: A tentativa de garantir o controle dos recursos naturais da Amazônia para o grande capital, in, http://philip.inpa.gov.br/publ_livres/Dossie/Mad/Outros%20documentos/As%2 0IFMs%20e%20o%20Complexo%20Rio%20Madeira.pdf. Accessed on 03/07/2015.

[71] GRIFFITHS, Tom, **Indigenous peoples and the World Bank: experiences with participation**, Indigenous Peoples Program, Forests Peoples Program: Moreton-in-Marsh, 2005, passim.

[72] DAVIS, Shelton H. **The World Bank and Indigenous Peoples**, The World Bank, 1993, passim.

Bank studies ironically happened at a time when the indigenous peoples started to formulate strong criticism of the integrationism that laid the grounds for the Convention and for the Bank's own studies. At the same time, and as a response to that critique, the ILO began to consider a general revision of Convention 107, which was actually carried out with the subsequent issuing of Convention 169.

OMS 2.34 was aimed at projects that could have an impact on 'tribal' populations, which was a recurring term in Convention 107. Tribal populations, according to the World Bank, were formed by stable ethnic groups with low energy consumption in their economic systems and that, in varying degrees, exhibited the following characteristics: (i) geographically isolated or semi-isolated, (ii) unacculturated or only partially acculturated into the societal norms of the dominant society, (iii) non monetized, or only partially monetized; production largely for subsistence, and independent of the national economic system, (iv) ethnically distinct from the national society, (v) nonliterate and without a written language, (vi) linguistically distinct from the wider society, (vii) identifying closely with one particular territory, (viii) having an economic lifestyle largely dependent on the specific natural environment, (ix) possessing indigenous leadership, but little or no national representation, and few, if any, political rights as individuals or collectively, partly because they do not participate in the political process; and (x) having loose tenure over their traditional lands, which for the most part is not accepted by the dominant society nor accommodated by its courts; and, having weak enforcement capabilities against encroachers, even when tribal areas have been delineated.

While the Bank policy recognized that it was the responsibility of governments to implement measures that will "effectively safeguard the integrity and well-being of the tribal people," it also stated that it would not support policies at either extreme: "either those that perpetuate isolation from the national society and needed social services; or, those promoting forced, accelerated acculturation unsuited to the future well-being of the affected tribal people. Finally, the World Bank's policies towards the projects it financed should be based upon detailed, contemporary knowledge of the peoples to be affected, considering: (i) the recognition, demarcation and protection of tribal areas containing those resources required to sustain the tribal people's traditional means of livelihood; (ii) appropriate social services that are consonant with the tribe's acculturation status, including, especially, protection against diseases and the maintaining of health; (iii) the maintenance, to the extent desired by the tribe, of its cultural integrity and embodiments thereof; and (iv) a forum for the participation of the tribal people in decisions affecting them, and providing for adjudication and redress of grievances.

A review of OMS 2.34 was carried out in 1989, that was based on the analysis of 33 projects financed by the World Bank between 1982 and 1986. Initially, it identified that the policies implemented by the World Bank assumed that rural populations were basically identical, which proved to be wrong. The 1983 analysis demonstrated that 15 projects impacted tribal areas: 36 in 1984 and 53 in 1986. Those projects, as revealed, focused on areas inhabited by small isolated non-acculturated tribal groups, who were therefore very vulnerable in view of the dimension of the projects and the economic interests involved. The review also identified that a large part of the projects didn't involve all the four protective measures determined by the Bank.

The revision of policies culminated in the issuing of Operational Directive 4.20 (OD 4.20) 'Indigenous Peoples' in 1991. At first, a change was made to the criterion for the identification of 'indigenous peoples', which came to mean social groups with a social and cultural identity distinct from the dominant society that makes them vulnerable to being disadvantaged in the development process. Similarly, OD 4.20 found that the denomination 'indigenous peoples' encompasses very diverse realities, which makes indigenous peoples identifiable only through certain characteristics, such as: (i) close attachment to ancestral territories and to the natural resources in these areas; (ii) self-identification and identification by others as members of a distinct cultural group; (iii) an indigenous language, often different from the national language; (iv) presence of customary social and political institutions; and (v) primarily subsistence-oriented production.

The Directive recognizes the need to protect indigenous peoples from potential harmful effects of development projects, as well as to grant them the opportunity - if they desire - to participate in the benefits of the development process. It was also established that there is a need for projects that are financed by the World Bank to be preceded by an analysis of its environmental impact, in the event that the project causes a significant impact on the environment. Finally, the directive indicates two relevant measures the Bank will take: (i) assistance to borrowers to enable and increase their ability to respond to indigenous claims; and (ii) the incorporation of indigenous issues into the Bank's policies, with the demand that borrowers must establish Programmes for the Development of Indigenous Peoples in the projects to be financed.

OD 4.20 was replaced by the Operational Manual - Indigenous Peoples OP/BP 4.10 in 2005. It maintained several aspects of OD 4.20, especially those related to the requirements to avoid the adverse impacts of the projects and to guarantee culturally appropriated benefits, and it strengthened the increase of participation by indigenous peoples in the projects that impact their territories. The great novelty of the new regulation is the requirement of Free, Prior, and Informed Consultation, and also the broad community support for the proposed project.

The regulation recognizes that, due to large projects, indigenous peoples are submitted to great risks, such as loss of cultural identity, way of life, of natural resources that are essential to their livelihood, etc. The new policy seeks to systematically encompass the problems indigenous peoples experience in order to exercise human rights in a manner consistent with their specific cultural characteristics and expressions of will. Additionally, the policy aims to ensure a development process that entirely respects the dignity, human rights, economy and culture of indigenous peoples. The OP/BP goals are also (i) to avoid potentially adverse impacts on indigenous peoples, and, if unavoidable, (ii) minimize, mitigate, or compensate for them.

Given the difficulties of identifying indigenous people and the lack of consensus on the issue, the Bank's policy employs the generic understanding of the term 'Indigenous Peoples', to refer to groups that are distinct from society and are culturally and socially vulnerable, who self-identify as indigenous, who have an indigenous language, and are recognized as such. Furthermore, they have a relation with the natural resources of their territory and have their own institutions, different from those of the national society. The World Bank applies these criteria regardless of the national legislation of the borrower's country.

There is also the requirement to document Free, Prior, and Informed Consultation, to demonstrate the broad communitary support of the indigenous peoples affected by the proposed project. The consultation process must be carried out according to the framework stipulated by Convention 169, that is, it should be

(i) culturally appropriate,
(ii) representative,
(iii) undertaken in good faith,
(iv) encompassing the many stages of the project,
(v) in the indigenous language,
(vi) with enough time to build consensus and
(vii) in places that allow for a large influx of indigenous peoples.

It is important to note that there is no definition of what should be understood by 'broad community support', meaning it is understood on a case-by-case basis. It is up to the Bank to review the procedures employed in the consultation stage, to evaluate the validity of the consultation. If the opinion of the financial institution is not in favour of the employed procedure, the loan process is suspended.

1.2 International Finance Corporation

As one of the institutions that make up the World Bank Group, the International Finance Corporation has developed mechanisms to manage the social and environmental risks of the projects it finances, such as the World Bank has done for itself. The IFC adopts the so-called

Performance Standards, of which no. 7[73] addresses issues related to indigenous and tribal peoples. The IFC makes use of a Sustainability Framework that aims to introduce the different social-environmental sustainability issues of the projects it finances as an important instrument for risk analysis.

Performance Standard no. 7 acknowledges that indigenous and tribal peoples are among the 'most marginalized and vulnerable segments of the population'. It also acknowledges that in many cases, their economic, social, and legal status limits their capacity to defend their rights to, and interests in, lands and natural and cultural resources, and may restrict their ability to participate in and benefit from development.

> "As a consequence, Indigenous Peoples may be more vulnerable to the adverse impacts associated with project development than non-indigenous communities. This vulnerability may include loss of identity, culture, and natural resource-based livelihoods, as well as exposure to impoverishment and diseases."[74]

The criteria to identify Indigenous and Tribal Peoples is generally adopted in the same way by Convention 169 and by OP/BP 4.10, without remarkable novelties.

It is up to the borrower to take the necessary measures to:

- Avoid Adverse Impacts: through an assessment process of all Indigenous and Tribal Peoples within the project area of influence who may be affected by the project, as well as the nature and degree of the expected direct and indirect economic, social, cultural, and environmental impacts on them.
- Participation and Consent: the client will undertake an engagement process with the Affected Communities of Indigenous Peoples as required in Performance Standard 1, which must include (i) stakeholder analysis and engagement planning, disclosure of information, consultation, and

[73] https://www.ifc.org/wps/wcm/connect/586227004d08289a99cbddf81ee631cc/PS7_ Portuguese_2012.pdf?MOD=AJPERES. Accessed on 17/10/2017.
[74] IFC, Padrão de Desempenho 7, p. 1.

participation, in a culturally appropriate manner, with the purpose of (a) involving Indigenous Peoples' representative bodies and organizations, (b) providing sufficient time for Indigenous Peoples' decision-making processes. Given the vulnerability of Indigenous and Tribal Peoples, the client will obtain Free, Prior, and Informed Consent of the Affected Communities, in the circumstances described in paragraphs 13-17 of the Performance Standard 7.[75]

[75] 13. Indigenous Peoples are often closely tied to their lands and related natural resources. Frequently, these lands are traditionally owned or under customary use. While Indigenous Peoples may not possess legal title to these lands as defined by national law, their use of these lands, including seasonal or cyclical use, for their livelihoods, or cultural, ceremonial, and spiritual purposes that define their identity and community, can often be substantiated and documented. 14. If the client proposes to locate a project on, or commercially develop natural resources on lands traditionally owned by, or under the customary use of, Indigenous Peoples, and adverse impacts can be expected, the client will take the following steps: (i) Document efforts to avoid and otherwise minimize the area of land proposed for the project; (ii) Document efforts to avoid and otherwise minimize impacts on natural resources and natural areas of importance to Indigenous People; (iii) Identify and review all property interests and traditional resource uses prior to purchasing or leasing land; (iv) Assess and document the Affected Communities of Indigenous Peoples' resource use without prejudicing any Indigenous Peoples' land claim. The assessment of land and natural resource use should be gender inclusive and specifically consider women's role in the management and use of these resources; (v) Ensure that Affected Communities of Indigenous Peoples are informed of their land rights under national law, including any national law recognizing customary use rights; and (vi) Offer Affected Communities of Indigenous Peoples compensation and due process in the case of commercial development of their land and natural resources, together with culturally appropriate sustainable development opportunities, including: - Providing land-based compensation or compensation-in-kind in lieu of cash compensation where feasible. - Ensuring continued access to natural resources, identifying the equivalent replacement resources, or, as a last option, providing compensation and identifying alternative livelihoods if project development results in the loss of access to and the loss of natural resources independent of project land acquisition. - Ensuring fair and equitable sharing of benefits associated with project usage of the resources where the client intends to utilize natural resources that are central to the identity and livelihood of Affected Communities of Indigenous People and their usage thereof exacerbates livelihood risk. - Providing Affected Communities of Indigenous Peoples with access, usage, and transit on land it is developing subject to overriding health, safety, and security considerations. 15. The client will consider feasible alternative project designs to avoid the relocation of Indigenous Peoples from communally held lands and natural resources subject to traditional ownership or under customary use.

- When any of these circumstances apply, the client will engage external experts to assist in the identification of the project risks and impacts.
- Since there is no universally accepted definition of Free, Prior, and Informed Consent, the IFC adopts the meaning described in paragraph 12 of Performance Standard 7. To sum up, it must: (i) be documented (ii) mutually agreed between the affected parties, (iii) provide evidence of agreement between the parties (iv) not require unanimity within the affected community.

1.3 Equator Principles

After the institutions that make up the World Bank adopted the aforementioned measures, the private sector also took the same track, inspired, above all, by the decisions taken by the International Finance Corporation, and created the Equator Principles. The Equator Principles are supported by 91 financial institutions in 37 countries[76] on all continents.[77] The Equator Principles are voluntary commitments

If such relocation is unavoidable the client will not proceed with the project unless FPIC has been obtained as described above. Any relocation of Indigenous Peoples will be consistent with the requirements of Performance Standard 5. Where feasible, the relocated Indigenous Peoples should be able to return to their traditional or customary lands, should the cause of their relocation cease to exist. 16. Where a project may significantly impact on critical cultural heritage that is essential to the identity and/or cultural, ceremonial, or spiritual aspects of Indigenous Peoples lives, priority will be given to the avoidance of such impacts. Where significant project impacts on critical cultural heritage are unavoidable, the client will obtain the FPIC of the Affected Communities of Indigenous Peoples. 17. Where a project proposes to use the cultural heritage including knowledge, innovations, or practices of Indigenous Peoples for commercial purposes, the client will inform the Affected Communities of Indigenous Peoples of (i) their rights under national law; (ii) the scope and nature of the proposed commercial development; (iii) the potential consequences of such development; and (iv) obtain their FPIC. The client will also ensure fair and equitable sharing of benefits from commercialization of such knowledge, innovation, or practice, consistent with the customs and traditions of the Indigenous Peoples.

[76] http://www.equator-principles.com/index.php/members-reporting, Accessed on 18/10/2017.

[77] The Brazilian banks integrating the Equator Principles are: Banco Bradesco, Banco do Brasil, Banco Votorantim, Caixa Econômica Federal, and Itaú Unibanco. There are several other international banks operating in Brazil that integrate the Equator Principles.

made by the institutions that adhere to them, to use them as "a risk management framework, adopted by financial institutions, for determining, assessing and managing environmental and social risk in projects". Nowadays, the Equator Principles III are in effect, for there is a mechanism of periodic content review in order to adapt to new realities. Regarding the subject of our work, the current revision, EP III, was carried out to adapt it to IFC norms, especially Performance Standard 7.

There are 10 (ten) principles: (i) Review and Categorisation, (ii) Environmental and Social Assessment, (iii) Applicable Environmental and Social Standards, (iv) Environmental and Social Management System and Equator Principles Action Plan, (v) Stakeholder Engagement (vi) Grievance Mechanism, (vii) Independent Review, (viii) Covenants, (ix) Independent Monitoring and Reporting (x) Reporting and Transparency. Such principles are applied in credit analysis to be offered to possible borrowers by the institutions linked to the EP.

> According to Exhibit I, it is understood that:
>
> "Environmental and Social Assessment (Assessment) is a process that determines the potential environmental and social risks and impacts (including labour, health, and safety) of a proposed Project in its area of influence."[78]
>
> "Affected Communities are local communities, within the Project's area of influence, directly affected by the Project."
>
> "Informed Consultation and Participation is an in-depth exchange of views and information and an organised and iterative consultation that leads the client to incorporate the views of Affected Communities, on issues that affect them directly (such as proposed mitigation measures, the sharing of development benefits and opportunities, and implementation issues), into their decision-making process."[79]
>
> Environmental and Social Assessment Documentation (Assessment Documentation) is a series of documents prepared for a Project as

[78] EP III, Appendix I, p. 18.
[79] EP III, Appendix 1, p. 19.

part of the Assessment process. The extent and detail of the documentation is commensurate with the Project's potential environmental and social risks and impacts. Examples of Assessment Documentation are: an Environmental and Social Impact Assessment (ESIA), Environmental and Social Management Plan (ESMP), or documents more limited in scale (such as an audit, risk assessment, hazard assessment and relevant project-specific environmental permits). Non-technical environmental summaries can also be used to enhance the Assessment Documentation when these are disclosed to the public as part a broader Stakeholder Engagement process.[80]

Stakeholder Engagement refers to IFC Performance Standards provisions on external communication, environmental and social information disclosure, participation, informed consultation, and grievance mechanisms. For the Equator Principles, Stakeholder Engagement also refers to the overall requirements described under Principle 5.[81]

Environmental and Social Impact Assessment (ESIA) is a comprehensive document of a Project's potential environmental and social risks and impacts. An ESIA is usually prepared for greenfield developments or large expansions with specifically identified physical elements, aspects, and facilities that are likely to generate significant environmental or social impacts. Exhibit II provides an overview of the potential environmental and social issues addressed in the ESIA.[82]

[80] EP III, Appendix I, p. 19.
[81] EP III, Appendix I, pp. 19-20.
[82] EP III, Appendix I, p. 20.

Comparison between EP II and EP III[83]

Changes to align with IFC's Performance Standards		
TOPIC	**EP II**	**EP III**
Social aspects	Social Risks Assessment Free, Prior, and Informed Consultation	Social and relevant Human Rights Assessment "Free, Prior, and Informed Consent" in specific circumstances Specific reference in the Preamble to assess Human Rights issues. Reference to the 'Guiding Principles on Business and Human Rights, Implementing the UN Protect, Respect and Remedy Framework'.
Language alignment	Environmental and Social Risks	Environmental and Social Risks and Impacts

The entire process must be consistent with the guidelines derived from the international treaties and conventions related to Indigenous and Tribal Peoples, as well as with the abundant jurisprudence on the matter, therefore, it must be free from external manipulation, interferences, coercion, or intimidation.

The documentation to be provided to the Affected Communities must be "readily accessible", and it's relevant to observe that it must be "culturally appropriate" and in the "local language".

It is important to remark that the signatory institutions of the Equator Principles "recognise that indigenous peoples may represent vulnerable segments of project-affected communities." In the case of projects that impact indigenous peoples, the client must make sure there has been a process of Informed Consultation and Participation, and that it will need to comply with the rights and protections for indigenous peoples contained in relevant national law, including those

[83] http://www.equator-principles.com/index.php/ep3/ep3, Accessed on 18/10/2017.

laws implementing host country obligations under international law. Consistent with the special circumstances described in IFC Performance Standard 7 (when relevant as defined in Principle 3). Thus, whenever there is a loan to be granted by a financial institution that is part of the Equator Principles, and the project has negative impacts on indigenous communities, there will be a requirement for Free, Prior, and Informed Consent.

CHAPTER 4

Indigenous and tribal peoples in South America

Introduction

In this section we aim to present a general overview of the indigenous and tribal peoples of South America who are subject to the protection offered by the legislation we are examining in this work. The different indigenous and tribal peoples on the South American Continent will be presented to the reader, as well as the demographic weight of each of these communities in their countries. Of course the complexity of the matter only allows for a generic view on the populations, without further elaboration on each one of them.

1 South American Countries

1.1 Argentina

The Argentinian Constitution,[84] following the tendency of other South American constitutions, established in Article 75, 17, that the National Congress is responsible for "recognizing the ethnic and cultural pre-existence of the Argentinian indigenous peoples", as well as guaranteeing respect for their identity and the right to a bilingual intercultural education, and also recognizing the legal personality of its

[84] http://servicios.infoleg.gob.ar/infolegInternet/anexos/0-4999/804/norma.htm, Accessed on 26/06/2017.

communities. It also ensures communitary ownership and possession of their traditionally occupied lands. The National Congress is also in charge of regulating the handing over of other lands that are suitable and sufficient for the human development of indigenous peoples. Indigenous lands in Argentina are inalienable and cannot be embargoed. Finally, the Constitution ensures that indigenous peoples participate in the management of natural resources in their territories. The legislative competence in indigenous matters in the federal government and the provinces is concurrent.

The fact that the Argentinian Constitution made an express mention of Argentinian indigenous peoples is important, because that nation has been struggling to recognize its 'Creole and American'[85] past as a foundation of its cultural roots. In Argentina, 35 indigenous peoples[86] are recognized, the vast majority located in the Salta Province, reaching a population of about one million people. Nine of the Argentinian indigenous ethnicities have their territories in Salta. The Argentinian State officially recognizes the existence of the following indigenous peoples: Atacama, Ava Guaraní, Aymara, Comechingón, Chané, Charrúa, Chorote, Chulupí, Diaguita-Calchaquí, Guaraní, Huarpe, Kolla, Lule, Mapuche, Mbyá Guaraní, Mocoví, Omaguaca, Ocloya, Pampa, Pilagá, Rankulche, Quechua, Querandí, Sanavirón, Selknam (Onas), Tapiete, Tehuelche, Tilián, Qom, Tonocoté, Tupí Guaraní, Vilela y Wichí, amongst others.[87] As in other countries in South America, Argentinian indigenous peoples experience a process of ethnogenesis, given the most favourable constitutional and legal conditions. Argentinian Indigenous Peoples are legally acknowledged in Law no. 23.302 of 1985 and, in accordance with legal provisions the legal personality of indigenous peoples in Argentina is recognized.

For legal purposes, the indigenous community is the group of families that recognize themselves as indigenous due to the fact that they descend from populations that inhabited the Argentinian territory at

[85] TARAGÓ, Myriam Noemi. **Los Pueblos Originarios y La Conquista.** First edition. Buenos Aires: Sudamericana, 2014, Kindle Edition.

[86] http://www.iwgia.org/regiones/latin-america/argentina, Accessed on 12/07/2017.

[87] http://www.territorioindigena.com.ar/Pueblos-Originarios, Accessed on 26/06/2017.

the time of the conquest or colonization, and indigenous or 'indians' are the members of such communities. According to the National Institute of Indigenous Affairs – INAI, each of these peoples have their own language, traditions, and culture.

1.2 Bolivia[88]

The Bolivian Constitution, in Article 30, broadly elaborates on indigenous peoples' rights (Originary Indigenous and Peasant Peoples) establishing a wide range of rules that spread from the cultural field to that of property rights. Bolivia is one of the Latin-American countries with the largest share of indigenous peoples in its population. According to the 2001 census, they reach up to 66,2% of the total national population, that is 6.529.213 people out of a total of 9.862.860. In the Andean country there are 39 different indigenous ethnic groups, the most numerous of them, Quechua and Aymara, are located in the highland; the Guaranis, Chiquitanos and Mojeños are located in the Amazon, whereas the other peoples are located in the lowlands (Guaranis, Chiquitanos, Moxeños, Guarayos, Movimas Chimanes, Itonamas and Tacanas, Reyesano, Yuracare, Joaquinianos and Weenhayek, Cavineños, Mosetén, Loretano, Ayoreos, Cayubaba, Chácobo, Baure, Canichana and Esse-ejja, Sirionó, Yaminahuas, Machineri, Yuki, Moré, Araona, Tapiete, Guarasugwe, Huaracaje, Pacahuara, Maropa and Leco).[89] The two largest indigenous ethnicities are (1) Aymara and (2) Quechua. The Aymara community has over 1.200.000 people, whereas the Quechuas makes up about 2.600.000 people, according to the 2001 census.

On 7 February 2009, Bolivia adopted a new Constitution that establishes in Article 1 that Bolivia is a "Unitary Social State of Plurinational, Community-Based Law", which is "free, independent, sovereign, democratic, intercultural, decentralized, and with

[88] http://www.mibolivia.net/36-etnias-de-bolivia-pueblos-indigenas/, Accessed on 26/06/2017.
[89] http://www.iwgia.org/regiones/latin-america/guatemala/64-esp-paises/bolivia/561-pueblos-indigenas-de-bolivia-hoy, Accessed on 26/06/2017.

autonomies". It is relevant to note that Article 2 of the Bolivian Constitution guarantees indigenous and peasant peoples their "free determination", that consists of their "right to autonomy, to self-government, their culture, recognition of their institutions, and the consolidation of their territorial entities", according to the Constitution and the laws. Article 5, I of the Bolivian Constitution recognizes the following official languages, Castilian and all the languages of the rural native indigenous nations and peoples, namely: Aymara, Araona, Baure, Bésiro, Canichana, Cavineño, Cayubaba, Chácobo, Chimán, Ese Ejja, Guaraní, Guarasu'we, Guarayu, Itonama, Leco, Machajuyai-kallawaya, Machineri, Maropa, Mojeño-Trinitario, Mojeño-Ignaciano, Moré, Mosetén, Movima, Pacawara, Puquina, Quechua, Sirionó, Tacana, Tapiete, Toromona, Uru-Chipaya, Weenhayek, Yaminawa, Yuki, Yuracaré, and Zamuco.

1.3 Chile

The Chilean Constitution originated in Pinochet's regime and doesn't recognize specific rights of Chilean indigenous peoples, even though there is an important aboriginal population in the Andean country. The Chilean government recognizes nine ethnic groups that represent more than one million people, or about 8% of the country's total population.[90] The norm that governs indigenous affairs in Chile is Law nº 19.253, of 1993.[91] According to the law, the indigenous are those who (i) have an indigenous mother or father, whatever the nature of the filiation, including adoption; (ii) are the descendents of indigenous ethnicities inhabiting the national territory, as long as they have at least one indigenous surname; (iii) maintain indigenous cultural traits, meaning the the ethnic groups' practice of modes of living, customs, or religion, in a habitual way or because one's spouse is indigenous, in which case it is necessary that they self-identify as indigenous.

[90] http://www.iwgia.org/regiones/latin-america/chile, Accessed on 26/06/2017.
[91] http://www.leychile.cl/Navegar?idNorma=30620, Accessed on 26/06/2017.

There is public and legal recognition of the following ethnicities: indigenous (Mapuche, Aymara, Rapa Nui or Pascuenses), Atacaman communities (Atacameñas, Quechuas, Collas and Diaguita from the north of the country, the Kawashkar or Alacalufe communities, and Yámana or Yagán from the southern channels).

1.4 Colombia

Colombia has a strong tradition of indigenous and Afro-Colombian populations, the latter being more numerous than the former. The Colombian constitution, as many others in South America, has several clauses about the protection of the rights of indigenous, Afro-Colombian, and other traditional communities. The indigenous population in Colombia is estimated at a million and a half people, or about 3,4% of the country's entire population. The Afro-descendent population is approximately 4.377.996 people, which makes up about 10,5% of the national population. Gypsies and Romani form about 0,01 % of the national population. About 80% of the indigenous population is concentrated in the Andes and in La Guajira.[92] (IWGIA, 2016).

Sixty-five indigenous languages are spoken in Colombia, 24 of which are suffering severe threats of extinction. Colombia boasts an extensive legislation designed to protect ethnic minorities, that is not restricted to specific protection of indigenous peoples.[93]

The different ethnicities recognized in Colombia are the following:[94] Achagua, Amorúa, Andoke, Arhuaco, Awa, Bara, Barasana, Barí, Betoye, Bora, Cañamomo, Carapana, Chimila; Chiricoa, Cocama, Coconuco, Coreguaje, Coyaima, Desano, Dujos, Embera, Embera Chamí, Embera Katio, Eperara Siapidara, Guambiano, Guanaca,

[92] International Work Group for Indigenous Affairs (IWGIA), **The Indigenous World**, Copenhagen: IWGIA, 2016, p. 120.

[93] http://www.urosario.edu.co/jurisprudencia/catedra-viva-intercultural/ur/Legislacion-colombiana-para-comunidades-etnicas/, Accessed on 28/06/2017.

[94] http://www.todacolombia.com/etnias-de-colombia/grupos-indigenas/distribucion.html, Accessed on 21/10/2017.

Guanes, Guayabero, Hitnu, Inga, Kankuamo, Karijona, Kawiyarí, Kofán, Kogui, Kubeo, Kuiba, Kurripako, Letuama, Makaguaje, Makuna, Matapí, Masiguare, Miraña, Mokana Muisca, Nasa, Nonuya, Nukak, Piratapuyo, Ocaina, Pasto, Piapoco, Piaroa, Piratapuyo, Pisamira, Puinave, Sáliba, Senú, Sicuani, Sikuane, Sikuani, Siona, Siriano, Taiwano, Tanimuka, Tariano, Tatuyo, Tikuna, Totoró, Tsiripu, Tucano, Tule, Tuyuka, U´wa, Uitoto, Wanano, Waunan, Wayuu, Wiwa, Yagua, Yanacona, Kamëntsa, Yaruros, Yauna, Yukuna, Yeral, Yuko, Yuri, and Yurutí.

1.5 Ecuador

Ecuador is one of the South-American countries that innovated the most when it comes to incorporating elements of autochtone and African-descendent cultures (Afro-Ecuadorian) in its Magna Carta. First of all, we must note the adoption of the concept of "Buen Vivir" (to live well) [Sumak Kawsay], a term that appears over twenty times in the Constitution and is one of the preambular objectives of the Ecuadorian constitutional order, it even has its own title. Similarly, we cannot fail to recognize the pioneering declaration of nature's own rights, which are considered in the Ecuadorian constitution (article 71, *La naturaleza o Pacha Mama, donde se reproduce y realiza la vida, tiene derecho a que se respete integralmente su existencia y el mantenimiento y regeneración de sus ciclos vitales, estructura, funciones y procesos evolutivos...* [Nature, or Pacha Mama, where life reproduces and generates itself, has the right of an integral respect for its existence, maintenance, and regeneration of its life cycles, structure, functions, and evolutionary processes...]).

Ecuador has a population of approximately 16 million people, with the following ethnical composition:

Mestizos	Montubios	Afro-Ecuadorians	Indigenous	Whites	Other
71.9%	7,4%	7,2%	7%	6,1%	0,3%

The Ecuadorian state recognizes the existence of thirteen[95] indigenous nationalities - divided into peoples - that are present in the three geopolitical regions of the country, each maintaining their own language, culture, and customs. In addition, there are isolated peoples, such as the Tagaeri, the Taromenane, and the Oñamenane peoples in the Amazon region.

In the last thirty years Ecuador has gone through two constituent processes that materialized in the Constitutions of 1998 and 2008, both with a vast recognition of the rights of traditional communities.

The different Ecuadorian ethnicities are distributed among the several Ecuadorian regions.[96] The Achuar, Andoa, Cofán, Secoya, Sinoa, Shiwiar, Shuar, Waorani and Zápra *nationalities* are located in the Amazon region, as are the Amazonian Kichwa peoples and uncontacted peoples. In the Costa region there are the Awá, Chachi, Épera, and Tsáchila nationalities, as well as the Manta-Huankavilka-Puná, Montubio, and Wankabilka peoples; in the Sierra region is home to the Kichwa nationality and the Chibuleo, Kañari, Karanki, Kayambi, Kisapincha, Kitu Kara, Natabuela, Otavalo, Palta, Panzaleo, Pasto, Puruwá, Salasaka, Saraguro, Tomabela, and Waranka peoples.

1.6 Guyana

Guyana is one of the youngest countries in South America, having gained its independence from the United Kingdom in May 1966. The country has a small multi-ethnic population composed of about 740.000 people, of whom 5,3% are indigenous, 30,5% African descendents, 51,4% Indian, 0,2% Chinese, 2,1% white, and 10% mestizo.[97] The Constitution of Guyana recognizes the right to protection and

[95] http://www.siise.gob.ec/siiseweb/PageWebs/glosario/ficglo_napuin.htm, Accessed on 26/06/2017.

[96] http://14nacionalidadesy18gruposetnicos.blogspot.com.br/2013/04/nacionalidades-y-pueblos-de-la-region.html, Accessed on 12/10/2017.

[97] http://www.hartford-hwp.com/archives/41/318.html, Accessed on 12/10/2017.

preservation of the languages, cultures, traditions, and modes of living of indigenous peoples (Article 149 G).[98]

There are nine indigenous peoples in Guyana, namely[99]: (i) Wai Wai, (ii) Macushis, (iii) Patomonas, (iv) Arawaks, (v) Caribs, (vi) Wapishana, (vii) Arecunas, (viii) Akawaios, and (ix) Warraus, who are governed by the Amerindian Act of 2006,[100] which provides for a wide range of aspects and its application is the responsibility of the Ministry of Indigenous People's Affairs. Nevertheless, there is strong criticism against the decision given by the High Court of Guyana in 2013, which recognized the validity of the concession of mining rights on properly titled indigenous lands. The Court understood that the rights granted before the enactment of the Amerindian Law of 2006 are not subject to the new law's provisions.[101]

1.7 Paraguay

The Paraguayan Constitution of 1992, in line with the modern South American Constitutions, has a chapter entirely dedicated to indigenous peoples, recognizing their traditions, ethnic and cultural peculiarities, including with regard to their communitary property rights. The population that recognizes itself as indigenous in Paraguay is relatively small – 112.848 people in 6 million, – considering the total number of inhabitants of the country. Though it is small, the indigenous population is composed of nineteen peoples belonging to five different linguistic families. The indigenous peoples are governed by Law no. 904/81 (Statute of Indigenous Communities),[102]

[98] 149 G. Indigenous peoples shall have the right to the protection, preservation and promulgation of their languages, cultural heritage and way of life., in http://parliament.gov.gy/constitution.pdf, Accessed on 12/10/2017.

[99] https://moipa.gov.gy/amerindian-nations/, Accessed on 12/10/2017.

[100] http:// www.moipa.gov.gy/wp-content/uploads/2015/02/AMERINDIAN-ACT-2006.pdf Accessed on 12/10/2017.

[101] http://rightsandresources.org/en/blog/fpp-press-release-guyana-court-ruling-violates-indigenous-peoples-rights/#.Wd-kPTBv82x, Accessed on 12/10/2017.

[102] http://www.cultura.gov.py/marcolegal/ley-90481-estatuto-de-las-comunidades-indigenas , Accessed on 27/06/2017.

highlighting that "[the] settlement of indigenous communities will attend as much as possible to the current or traditional possession of lands. Free and express consent of the indigenous community will be essential to their settlement in places other than their usual territories, except in cases of national security", according to article 64 of the Paraguayan Constitution. It is worth noting the fact that approximately 90% of the Paraguayan population speaks Guarani language - almost 40% exclusively - ,[103] even though they do not recognize themselves as indigenous. Paraguayan indigenous peoples are divided into five linguistic groups: ((i) Guarani, (ii) Maskoy, (iii) Mataco-Mataguayo, (iv) Zamuco, and (v) Guaiacurú), and they are the following peoples: (i) Guarani Ñandeva, Pai Tavyterã, Mbya Guarani, Avá Guaraní, Aché; (ii) Guaná, Toba Maskoy (or Enenxet), Sanapaná, Angaité, Enxet and Enlhet, (iii) Nivaclé, Maká and Manjui, (iv) Ayoreode, Yshyro, and (v) Toba Qom (or Quom Lick).

1. 8 Suriname

Suriname is the youngest country of South America, having gained its independence from the Netherlands on 25 November 1975. The population of the country is approximately 541.638 people, with an indigenous population of about 3,8% in total. There are many ethnicities in Suriname,[104] the largest being the (i) Kali'ña (Caribs), (ii) the Lokono (Arawaks), (iii) the Trio (Tirio, Tareno), and (iv) the Wayana. Other numerically smaller ethnicities are (i) Akurio, (ii) Apalai, (iii) Wai-Wai, (iv) Katuena/Tunayana, (v) Mawayana, (vi) Pireuyana, (vii) Sikiiyana, (viii) Okomoyana, (ix) Alamayana, (x) Maraso, (xi) Sirewu, and (xii) Sakëta. Besides indigenous peoples, there are six tribal peoples present in Suriname (the Maroons): (i) Saramaka, (ii) N'djuka, (iii) Matawai, (iv) Kwinti, (v) Aluku, and (vi) Paramaka. The population of tribal peoples is about 117.500 people, or about 21% of the country's

[103] https://www.giz.de/fachexpertise/downloads/giz2010-es-laenderpapier-paraguay.pdf, Accessed on 27/06/2017.

[104] https://www.iwgia.org/images/documents/indigenous-world/indigenous-world-2017.pdf, Accessed on 12/10/2017.

population. The main case involving the rights of indigenous and tribal peoples that was examined by the Inter-American Court of Human Rights is from Suriname (the Saramaka Case), involving the Maroon community.

In historical terms, the Maroons are to Suriname what the quilombolas are to Brazil, because they are also mostly descendents of African slaves who rebelled against slavery and established communities in the country's forests in the seventeenth and eighteenth centuries.[105] However, Suriname is not a signatory of Convention 169 and also does not have any legislation protecting the rights of indigenous peoples. The official position adopted by the country is that the recognition of the rights of indigenous and tribal peoples would correspond to a denial of the same rights to other parts of the population. Therefore, the rights of indigenous and tribal peoples are not adequately protected in the country, as we can conclude from the extensive research undertaken by Ellen-Rose Kambel and Fergus Mackay.[106]

1.9 Uruguay

Uruguay is perhaps the South American country where the situation of indigenous peoples is the most paradoxical. The Uruguayan state has always had much difficulty in recognizing the existence of indigenous peoples in its territory, so much so that the demographic census carried out in 1996 only identified 12.600 people as "descendents of indigenous peoples".[107] In 2006, those who self-declared as indigenous descendents reached a total of 115.118 people, or 4% of the population

[105] https://www.forestpeoples.org/sites/fpp/files/publication/2015/07/suriname-shadow-2015-final.pdf, Accessed on 12/10/2017.

[106] KAMBEL, Ellen-Rose e MACKAY, Fergus. **The Rights of the Indigenous Peoples and Maroons in Suriname**, Copenhagen: IWGIA, 1999, passim.

[107] http://www.lr21.com.uy/comunidad/462619-en-uruguay-hay-115118-descendientes-de-indigenas, Accessed on 09/07/2017.

of the country. It is worth noting that Uruguay, along with Suriname, is not part of Convention 169.[108]

The Uruguayan Constitution doesn't have any norm protecting indigenous peoples, since they are considered to be non-existent in the country. However, even though they are lagging behind the other countries in South America, it seems evident that the 'resurgence' of indigenous peoples is a matter of time in Uruguay as well. It is believed – even if mythologically – that the Uruguayan indigenous people (the Charruas) were exterminated and made 'extinct' in the so-called Salsipuedes massacre, which took place where the border between the departments of Paisandú and Tacuarembó is today. The massacre was a killing of Charruas families who inhabited the region. It is a fact that deserves strong condemnation by the Uruguayan population. The consequence of the massacre was the extinction of the Charruas, with only a tiny portion of Charruas descendents left in the modern Uruguayan population.[109]

The Charruas massacre took place on 11 April 1831, carried out by troops under the command of Fructuoso Rivera. The actual number of Charruas killed was forty people, with 300 of them being held as prisoners. The conception that they were executed evidently played a role in Europeanizing the Uruguayan population, taking out the indigenous element. It is relevant to consider that in the mythology of the foundation of Uruguay as a nation, Artigas – the founder of the Uruguayan nation – is thought to be a friend of the Charruas.

With respect to the populations of African descent, Law no. 19.122[110] was approved in 2013 to promote so-called affirmative actions in favour of those populations, especially in the field of work relations. In the cultural sphere, Law no. 18.059 recognizes the Candombe and Afro-Uruguayan culture as heritage of the eastern nation. The

[108] http://www.ilo.org/dyn/normlex/en/f?p=NORMLEXPUB:11300:0::NO::P11300_I N STRUMENT_ID:312314, Accessed on 09/07/2017.

[109] http://www.todouruguay.net/el-fin-de-los-charruas-la-matanza-de-salsipuedes/, Accessed on 09/07/2017.

[110] https://legislativo.parlamento.gub.uy/temporales/leytemp6752166.htm, Accessed on 10/07/2017.

population census carried out in 2011 indicates the existence of about 256.000 Uruguayan citizens of African descent, that is, approximately 8,1 % of the national population.[111] Of all the South American countries, Uruguay, along with Chile, has the worst legislation for the protection of ethnic minorities.

1.10 Venezuela

Venezuela, as most South American countries, recognizes itself as multiethnic and multicultural, a condition that is expressed in its Constitution. The Venezuelan population is about 27 million inhabitants, of which 2,8 % are indigenous, according to the census of 2011. The African descendents correspond to about 21,75% of the national population. The recognized indigenous peoples in Venezuela are: Akawayo, Amorúa, Añú, Arawak, Arutani, Ayamán, Baniva, Baré, Barí, Caquetío, Cumanagoto, Chaima, E´ñepá, Gayón,, Guanano, Hoti, Inga, Japreria, Jirajara, Jivi, Kari´ña, Kubeo, Kuiva, Kurripako, Mako, Makushi, Nengatú, Pemón, Piapoko, Píritu, Puinave, Pumé, Sáliva, Sánema, Sapé, Timoto-cuica, Waikerí, Wanai, Wapishana, Warao, Warekena, Wayuu, Wotjuja, Yanomami, Yavarana, and Ye´kuana Yukpa.

The Constitution has a vast chapter about indigenous peoples (Chapter VII), in which the strong influence of Article 231 of the Brazilian Constitution can be felt.

Venezuela has extensive legislation for the protection of indigenous peoples, with emphasis on the following laws: (i) the Organic Law on Demarcation and Guarantee of the Habitat and Lands of Indigenous Peoples, (ii) Convention 169 of the International Labour Organization, (iii) the Organic Law on Indigenous Peoples and Communities, (iv) the United Nations Declaration on the Rights of Indigenous Peoples, (v) the Indigenous Languages Act, (vi) the Law for the Cultural Heritage of Indigenous Peoples, (vii) the Law for Indigenous Artisan and Art Crafts.

111 http://www.elpais.com.uy/opinion/editorial/afrodescendientes-casos-discriminacion-racial-editorial.html, Accessed on 10/07/2017.

CHAPTER 5

Brazilian communities protected by Convention 169

Introduction

At this point we shall present the Brazilian communities that can be classified as indigenous and tribal peoples for the specific purposes of applying Convention 169 and related legislation. Brazil is known to be a country of continental dimensions that is composed of different ethnic groups that constitute its people, as is expressly recognized by the Federal Constitution. According to the provisions in the first paragraph of Article 215 of the Federal Constitution, the state is responsible for protecting manifestations of popular, indigenous, and Afro-Brazilian cultures, as well as of "other groups participating in the national civilizational process", which explicitly admits a cultural and ethnic plurality in the cultural formation of our country. In the same way, with Article 216, the Constitution included in Brazilian cultural heritage "assets of a material and immaterial nature, taken individually or as a whole, which bear reference to the identity, action and memory of the various groups that form the Brazilian society", including (i) forms of expression and (ii) ways of creating, making, and living, among others.

The communities referred to in the constitutional rule, are in principle protected by Convention 169 and, according to data of the United Nations Development Programme, are composed of about five million people who occupy approximately a quarter of the national territory[112]. Besides indigenous peoples, other traditional communities are included in the comprehensive concept of tribal peoples. We must note that the Executive Power, in order to fulfil constitutional dictates, issued a series of decrees on the subject, the last one being Decree no. 6.40, of 7 February 2007, which institutes the National Policy of Sustainable Development of Traditional Peoples and Communities. According to the decree, "Traditional Communities and Peoples" are culturally differentiated groups that recognize themselves as such, having their own modes of social organization, and that occupy and use natural territories and resources for their cultural, social, religious, ancestral, and economic reproduction, using knowledge, innovations, and practices that are generated and transmitted through tradition.

It is important to observe that the legal definition is based on (i) a subjective concept: self-recognition of belonging to a different culture; and (ii) other concepts that are objective, such as their own forms of social organization, traditional occupation of territories and the use of natural resources as a condition for cultural, social, religious, ancestral and economic reproduction, using knowledge, innovation, and practices generated and transmitted through tradition. Both fundamental concepts are essential for the cultural characterization of those populations, otherwise there may be wrongful extension of the protection provided, which could subvert the concepts by trivializing them.

Traditional peoples and communities can occupy Traditional Territories that are, in the terms of the applicable norm, the necessary spaces for the cultural social, and economic reproduction of traditional peoples and communities, whether they are used permanently or temporarily, according to what is stated about indigenous and quilombola peoples in Article 231 of the Constitution and Article 68 of the Transitory Constitutional Provisions Act and other regulations.

For the purposes of applying the policy, sustainable development was defined as the balanced use of natural resources, aimed at the

[112] http://www.seppir.gov.br/comunidades-tradicionais/o-que-sao-comunidades-tradicionais, Accessed on 10/06/2017.

improvement of the quality of life of the current generation, guaranteeing the same possibilities for future generations.

1 Recognized traditional communities

With the Decree of 27 December 2004, the Brazilian State created the National Committee for Sustainable Development of Traditional Communities, with the purpose of (i) establishing the National Policy for Sustainable Development of Traditional Communities; (ii) supporting, proposing, evaluating, and harmonizing the principles and guidelines of public policy related to the sustainable development of traditional communities within the scope of the Federal Government; (iii) proposing public policy actions for the implementation of the National Policy for Sustainable Development of Traditional Communities, considering the social and economical dimensions, and ensuring the sustainable use of natural resources; (iv) proposing measures of articulation and harmonization of sectorial, state and municipal public policies, as well as activities for the implementation of the National Policy goals for Sustainable Development of Traditional Communities, encouraging the decentralized execution of such actions; (v) articulating and proposing actions for the implementation of such policies, as a means to attend to situations that require special measures or are emergencial; (vi) monitoring the implementation of the National Policy for Sustainable Development of Traditional Communities within the scope of the Federal Government; (vii) suggesting criteria for the regulation of agro-extractivist activities; and (viii) proposing, supporting and accompanying the Federal Government's execution of strategies aimed at the development of agro-extractivism. The aforementioned Decree was partially revoked by the Decree of 13 July 2006, which altered the denomination, composition, and competence of the National Committee for the Development of Traditional Communities.

The National Committee for the Development of Traditional Communities[113] recognizes the existence of several traditional peoples

[113] http://portalypade.mma.gov.br/, Accessed on 10/06/2017.

and communities, namely: (i) andirobeiras, (ii) apanhadores de sempre-vivas, (iii) catingueiros, (iv) caiçaras, (v) castanheiras, (vi) catadores de mangaba, (vii) Roma (viii) cipozeiros, (ix) extrativistas, (x) faxinalenses, (xi) fundo e fecho de pasto, (xii) Geraizeiros, (xiii) Ilheus, (xiv) Indígenas, (xv) Isqueiros, (xvi) Morroquianos, (xvii) Pantaneiros, (xviii) Pescadores Artesanais, (xix) Piaçaveiros, (xx) Pomeranos, (xxi) Povos de Terreiro, (xxii) Quebradeiras de Coco de Babaçu, (xxiii) Quilombolas, (xxiv) Retireiros, (xxv) Ribeirinhos, (xxvi) Seringueiros, (xxvii) Vazanteiros, (xxviii) Veredeiros.

According to Article 1º, 1(a) of Convention 169, recognition 'by special legislation' suffices for the traditional population to be included among the possible beneficiaries of its terms. The federative nature of Brazil allows for the member states of the federation, in many cases, to recognize traditional populations that in the end may not have obtained federal recognition.

The traditional communities officially recognized by the Brazilian State certainly are not exhaustive of the specific universe, which may be much vaster, as there is a growing number of small rural communities that claim their recognition as a traditional community. This phenomenon has many origins and it certainly tends to expand, given the long process of social affirmation of communities that have been marginalized for a long period. Once they recognize themselves as a singular group they gain self-esteem and self-respect. However, the fact that these communities are very diverse cannot go unnoticed, and it is difficult to find a common ground between them all. The inclusion of indigenous peoples in this list, for instance, is pointless because they have their own originary rights both in Convention 169 and in the Brazilian Constitution, and they even have their own protective agency, FUNAI. The same goes for quilombolas [runaway slaves], which are also considered in the Federal Constitution with their own laws, and with the Palmares Foundation.

It is possible, however, to identify a tendency to include several poor urban and rural communities in the list of traditional communities, regardless of whether or not they fulfil the objective requirements of the C169 to be recognized as such. On the other hand, we cannot fail to acknowledge that, in the exact terms of Convention 169, legal recognition by the state generates tutelage, so that discussions about the sociological or anthropological nature of these communities is irrelevant when it comes to giving support by legal tutelage.

The Roma people[114] are of unknown origin, although they are believed to have originated in India and spread all around the world about one thousand years ago. It is recorded that the first Roma that landed in Brazil were a couple sentenced to a five year exile in Brazil.[115] The Federal Government's National Office for Policies for the Promotion of Racial Equality recognizes the existence of more than three gypsy ethnic groups in Brazil, (i) Calon, (ii) Roma and (iii) Sinti, each with their own language and ways of living.

It is estimated that the Roma population lives in about 291 Brazilian cities, in twenty-one states of the federation. Most of the Roma population is gathered in Minas Gerais, Bahia, and Goiás, in many settlements. The Brazilian Roma population is estimated at around 500.000 people.

2 Indigenous peoples

In Brazil there are about 254 indigenous or original peoples, of which approximately forty-eight have part of their population living in other countries.[116] The Brazilian indigenous population, according to the 2010 census, makes up 896.917 people, of which 324.834 live in cities and 572.083 in rural areas. The indigenous peoples do not even make up 1% of the Brazilian population.

[114] http://portalypade.mma.gov.br/ciganos, Accessed on 20/06/2017.

[115] http://www.seppir.gov.br/comunidades-tradicionais/copy_of_povos-de-cultura-cigana, Accessed on 20/06/2017.

[116] https://pib.socioambiental.org/pt/c/0/1/2/populacao-indigena-no-brasil, Accessed on 22/10/2017.

Indigenous Lands[117]

PROCESS PHASE	QUANTITY	SURFACE (ha)
Delimited	36	4.177.382,9358
Declared	73	3.415.646,6662
Approved	17	1.586.696,8980
Regularized	435	105.648.344,8943
TOTAL	**561**	**116.850.683,5021**
Studied	114	5.769,0000
Interdiction decree	6	1.084.049,0000

The Brazilian Constitution (Article 231) acknowledges 'the indians' social organization, customs, languages, beliefs and traditions, and their originary rights over the lands they traditionally occupy. It is the responsibility of the Union to demarcate and protect them, respecting all their assets". In addition, the second paragraph of said article attributes to the indigenous peoples the "exclusive use" of the riches of the soil, rivers, and lakes on indigenous lands.

The institution of indigenous constitutional usufruct clearly enforces that any activity that may be carried out on indigenous lands must have the prior consent of the indigenous peoples who inhabit them, and furthermore, they must participate in its earnings. Otherwise, the usufruct would be violated. It is important to stress that paragraph 6 of Article 231 disparages with annulment and extinction "*acts that aim at the occupation, dominion, and possession of lands...*" or the "*exploitation of the natural riches of their soil, rivers, and lakes*". Regarding this matter, the Federal Supreme Court has already decided that:

> The potential existence of a real estate registration in the name of a person, despite the provisions of Art. 859 of the 1916 Civil Code, or what is stated in Art. 1.245 and paragraphs of the current Civil Code, does not mean this private domain title is in opposition with

117 http://www.funai.gov.br/index.php/indios-no-brasil/terras-indigenas, Accessed on 22/10/2017.

> the Federal Union, for the Constitution of the Republic has pre-excluded indigenous lands *res extra commercium* from legal commerce, thus proclaiming null and declaring the extinction of acts that pursue the occupation, dominion, and possession of such areas, also considering ineffective business agreements that affect these lands, without any possibility for legal consequences, including those that provoke, as an effect of express constitutional refusal, the very denial of the right to compensation or of access to legal actions against the Federal Union, with the sole exception of benefactions derived from an occupation in good faith (FC, Art. 231, § 6). [RMS 29.193 AgR-ED, rel. min Celso de Mello, j. 16-12-2014, 2nd T, DJE of 19-2-2015.]

As a consequence of Articles 231 and 232 of the Federal Constitution, as well as the development of certain specific public policies, indigeneous populations have been growing at a pace that is greater than the national average, largely due to a process of ethnogenesis[118] and the restoration of indigenous pride. According to information from FUNAI,[119]

> "Since 1991, the IBGE [*Instituto Brasileiro de Geografia e Estatística* - Brazilian Institute of Geography and Statistics] has included indigenous peoples in the national demographic census. The number of Brazilians who considered themselves indigenous grew by 150% in the 1990s. The pace of the growth was six times higher than that of the general population. The percentage of indigenous peoples in relation to the total Brazilian population took a leap from 0,2% in 1991 to 0,4% in 2000, a total of 734 thousand people. There was an annual increase of 10,8% of the population, the highest growth rate among all categories, as the total growth average was 1,6%."

The Brazilian indigenous peoples[120] are: Aicanãs, Ajurus, Amanaiés, Amondauas, Anambés, Aparai, Apiacás, Apurinã, Arapaso, Arara, Araras-do-aripuanã, Aruás, Campas, Assurinis-do-Tocantins, Assurinis-

[118] BANTON, Michael. **A Ideia de Raça** (Translated by António Marques Bessa), Lisbon, Edições 70, 2015, passim.

[119] http://www.funai.gov.br/index.php/indios-no-brasil/quem-sao, Accessed on 10/06/2017.

[120] Non-exhaustive list.

do-xingu, Avás-canoeiros, Guajás, Auetis, Bacairis, Barás, Barasanas, Baré, Bororos, Chamacocos, Chiquitanos, Cintas-largas, Denis, Desanos, Enáuenês-nauês, Fulniôs, Gavião Mondé, Paracatejê-gavião, Pucobié-gavião, Guajajaras, Guaranis, Guatós, Hupda, Ikpeng, Ingarikó, Jabutis, Jamamadis, Jarauaras, Javaés, Jiahuis, Jumas, Kaapor, Caiabis, Caingangues, Caixanas, Calapalos, Camaiurás, Cambebas, Cambiuás, Canamaris, Apaniecras-canelas, Rancocamecras-canelas, Canindés, Canoês, Carajá, Karapanã, Karapotó, Karipuna, Caripunas-do-amapá, Cariris, Cariris-xocós, Caritianas, Araras-caros, Karuazu, Katukina, Katxuyana, Kaxarari, Kaxinawá, Kaxixó, Caiapós, Quiriris, Cocamas, Korubo, Craós, Krenaks, Cricatis, Kubeo, Kuikuro, Kulina Madihá, Culinas-pano, Kuripako, Curuaias, Kwazá, Macurap, Makuna, Macuxis, Matipus, Matis, Maxacalis, Meinacos, Miranha, Miritis-tapuias, Mundurucus, Muras, Nauquás, Nambiquaras, Nukini, Ofaiés, Oro-uins, Paiter, Palicures, Panará, Pancararés, Pankararu, Pankaru, Parakanã, Parecis, Parintintins, Patamona, Pataxó, Pipipãs, Pirarrãs, Piratapuias, Pitaguaris, Potiguaras, Poianauas, Ricbactas, Sakurabiat, Sateré-Mawé, Shanenawa, Suruís, Suiás, Tabajaras, Tapaiúnas, Tapirapés, Tapuias, Tarianas, Terenas, Ticunas, Tiriós, Torás, Truká, Trumai, Tsunhuns-djapás, Tucanos, Tumbalalá, Tuparis, Tupinambás, Tupiniquins, Tuiúcas, Umutinas, Uaimiris-atroaris, Uapixanas, Uarequenas, Uassus , Uaurás, Uaianas, Xakriabás, Xambioás, Xavantes, Xerentes, Xetás, Caiapós-xicrins, Xipaias, Xukuru, Xukuru Kariri, Yaminawa, Ianomâmis, Iaualapitis, Iecuanas, Jurunas, Zoés, Zorós and Suruuarrás.

3 Remaining quilombo population (Quilombolas)

Like the indigenous peoples, the Quilombolas deserved special and preferential treatment in the Brazilian Constitution. As such, the fifth paragraph of Article 215 determines the *registered heritage status* of all documents and places with historical reminiscences of the ancient quilombos. Article 68 of the Transitory Constitutional Provisions Act recognized the ownership of lands occupied by the remaining quilombos, leaving the state's responsible for issuing the respective titles. At this point, two observations can be made: (i) the ownership of quilombola land belongs to the quilombolas themselves - who are considered collectively - and not to the Union, as is the case with indigenous lands, according to Article 20, XI of the Federal Constitution. And (ii), both the federal state and the Union can issue the respective titles, the Union doesn't hold exclusive competence.

The quilombo remnants were recognized as local communities, as a "human group... distinguished by its cultural conditions, that organizes itself traditionally by successive generations and its own customs, and which preserves its social and economic institutions", as it is stated in Provisional Measure 2186-16, Article 7, III, later revoked by Law no. 13.123 of 28 May 2015, which deals with access to traditional knowledge associated with biological diversity.

In Brazil, 2958 remaining quilombo communities[121] have already been officially identified, with many recognitions and land titles.

3.1 Black Fugitives and Their Societies

As noted by Flávio dos Santos Gomes,[122] the colonization of the Americas was based on the compulsory labour of indigenous peoples and black Africans. Among the indigenous and black African peoples there were many different ethnicities "coming from micro-societies with decentralized power, like High Guinea and Senegambia, as well as from the empires and kingdoms of Daomé, Oyo, Ndongo, Ketu, Matamba and others; or from cities such as Uidá and Luanda, in western African areas, between savannas and forests".[123] Both the indigenous and African peoples did not passively accept captivity, and throughout the Americas there were rebellions and resistance to imprisonment and forced labour.

[121] http://www.palmares.gov.br/wp-content/uploads/2017/05/quadro-geral-15-05-2017.pdf, Accessed on 15/06/2017.

[122] GOMES, Flávio dos Santos. **Mocambos e Quilombos - Uma História do Campesinato Negro no Brasil**. São Paulo: Claroenigma, 2015, p. 8.

[123] For an excellent understanding of African diversity, see M`Bokolo, 2009.

The resistance to slavery – whether by indigenous or African peoples – gave rise to many communities of refugees which often joined together Africans, indigenous peoples, and whites. These communities, originating from slave runaways, according to Richard Price can be found "from Brazil to the south of the USA, from Peru to the American Southwest".[124] Communities of runaway African Americans were given various names in the Americas, such as the *cumbes* in Venezuela, *palenques* in Colombia; *Maroons* in Jamaica, the English Caribbean and south of the USA; *Bush negroes* in Suriname; *Cimarron* in the French Caribbean, Cuba and Puerto Rico.[125] Gomes reminds us that in Brazil, the communities were, "since the first decades of colonization... known firstly as *mocambos* and later as *quilombos*". Although they were predominantly composed of African-American runaways or their descendents, the quilombos were not limited to them. Research shows that there was an ethnic variety, with the presence of indigenous and white peoples. Quilombos are complex phenomena due to their origins, population, and even their insertion in the colonial economy.

The chart below shows the degree of miscegenation found in some Brazilian quilombos:

Genetic ancestry of quilombo inhabitants[126]

Name of the quilombo	African	European	Indigenous
Cametá (North)	48%	17,9%	34,1%
Cajueiro (Northeast)	67,4%	32,6%	0%
Curiaú (North)	73,6%	26,4%	0%
Paredão (South)	79,2%	2,8%	18,1%
Trombetas (North)	62%	27%	11%
Valongo (South)	97,3%	2,7%	0%
Mimbó (Northeast)	61%	17%	22%
Sítio Velho (Northeast)	72%	12%	16%

[124] PRICE, Richard. **Maroon Societies: Rebel Slave Communities in the Americas** (Ed.), New York: Anchor Book, 1973, Kindle Edition, position 65.

[125] GOMES, Flávio dos Santos. **Mocambos e Quilombos – Uma História do Campesinato Negro no Brasil**. São Paulo: Claroenigma, 2015, p. 10

[126] https://pt.wikipedia.org/wiki/Quilombo#cite_note-20, Accessed on 16/06/2017.

It is important to note that, just as the other traditional populations, the notion of territory is very important for the quilombolas, since the 'ownership' of the land is collective.[127] It should be observed that with the end of the slavery regime in Brazil, the formation of the quilombos was no longer restricted to refuge sites of runaways. According to Maria de Lourdes Bandeira's observations, "the lands where these African American rural communities settled their territory can be classified according to their heritage origins, donations from former masters and their slaves, donations to saints, and unclaimed lands."[128]

3.2 Identification of Remaining Quilombo Populations

The identification of the remaining quilombo population is a complex subject, because it involves the need for different types of studies, that are historical, anthropological, social, etc. To organize the matter, the Federal Government issued Decree no. 4.487 of 20 November 2003. The Decree was submitted to an unconstitutionality claim before the Federal Supreme Court (ADI 3239) on 25/08/2004. The reporting judge Minister Cezar Peluso (already retired) voted for the unconstitutionality of the Decree, a final judgement on the subject is awaited. The divergence was initiated by Minister Rosa Weber (25 March 2015), who requested adjournment for a case review on 8 April 2012. After the vote of Minister Rosa Weber there was another request for case review by Minister Dias Tófolli, the ADI still awaits a decision. From the vote of Minister Rosa Weber, the following deserves to be highlighted as indicated in notice 779 of the FSC:

> As a fully efficient rule with direct, immediate, and integral applicability, Article 68 of the ADCT would be able to produce all its effects when the Constitution enters into force, regardless of an infra-constitutional integrative norm. What is stated in Article 68 of

[127] BANDEIRA, Maria de Lourdes. **Terras Negras: invisibilidade expropriadora**, in, Textos e Debates, Year 1, no.o. 2, 1991, UFSC, p. 8.
[128] BANDEIRA, Maria de Lourdes. **Terras Negras: invisibilidade expropriadora**, in, Textos e Debates, Year 1, no. 2, 1991, UFSC, p. 8.

> the ADCT would configure an effective exercise of the regulatory power of the Administration, within the limits established by Article 84, IV and VI of the FC and, therefore, there would have been no harm to legality or the law. It made clear that the so- called quilombolas, traditional peoples whose historical contribution to the plural cultural formation of Brazil was recognized only in the 1988 Constitution, although they are not native as the indigenous peoples, they bear, like them, distinctive ethno-cultural features marked by a special socio-cultural relation with the occupied land: they became native and incorporated in the territorial environment. Thus, at the same time that, on the one hand it wouldn't be possible to arrive at a meaning for quilombo with an absolute rigidity, on the other hand, it also cannot be affirmed that the concept appearing in Article 68 of the ADCT would reach any and all predominantly Afro-descendant rural communities, without historical connection to the linguistic use of this term. Self-attribution as a criterion for determining quilombola identity would not be illegitimate before the constitutional order. It stresses that good-faith should be presumed and that no one could be denied the identity they atributte themselves and, as for bad-faith, administrative law would have appropriate measures.

However, it is worth pointing out that the demarcations and identifications of remaining quilombos have, for the most part, obtained judicial confirmation, given the majority understanding of self-applicability of Article 68 of the ADCT.

CHAPTER 6

The Inter-American System for the Protection of Human Rights; and free, prior, and informed consultation

Introduction

The so-called The Inter-American System for the Protection of Human Rights is a legal, administrative, and judicial structure primarily based on the Organization of American States in the different institutions that are linked to it. The origins of the OAS can be found in the First International Conference of American States[129] that took place in Washington from October 1889 to April 1890. The OAS was created in 1948 in Bogotá, Colombia. There are many legal documents in the sphere of the OAS that provide consistency to the defense of Human Rights at a hemispheric level, as previously seen.

The Conventions, Treaties, and Declarations that have been mentioned and addressed in this work, in order to exist in the real world, need an enforcement structure that is able to make them effective. On the American continent, the international implementation of such documents is the responsibility of the Inter-American System of Human Rights, led by the Inter-American Court of Human Rights. The enormous growth, in all South American countries, of legal and administrative demands proposed by indigenous and tribal peoples from the end of the 20th century onwards, was enhanced by the

[129] http://www.oas.org/es/acerca/quienes_somos.asp, Accessed on 23/10/2017.

institution of the Inter-American System for the Protection of Human Rights, whose milestone is the Pact of San Jose, Costa Rica. The main pillars of the System are (i) a legal structure and (ii) an administrative and legal structure.

Countries that are part of the Inter-American System of Human Rights[130]

Member States of the OAS	Signatories of the American Convention on Human Rights	Recognizing the competence of the Inter-American Court of Human Rights.
Antigua and Barbuda, Argentina, the Bahamas, Barbados, Belize, Bolivia, Brazil, Canada, Colombia, Costa Rica, Chile, Dominica, Ecuador, El Salvador, the United States, Granada, Guatemala, Guiana, Haiti, Honduras, Jamaica, Mexico, Nicaragua, Panama, Paraguay, Peru, Dominican Republic, Saint Kitts and Nevis, Santa Lucia, São Vicente and Granadinas, Suriname, Trinidad and Tobago, Uruguay, and Venezuela.	Argentina, Barbados, Bolivia, Brazil, Chile, Colombia, Costa Rica, Dominica, Ecuador, El Salvador, Granada, Guatemala, Haiti, Honduras, Jamaica, Mexico, Nicaragua, Panama, Paraguay, Peru, Dominican Republic, Suriname, Trinidad and Tobago, Uruguay, and Venezuela.	Argentina, Barbados, Bolivia, Brazil, Chile, Colombia, Costa Rica, Ecuador, El Salvador, Guatemala, Haiti, Honduras, Mexico, Nicaragua, Panama, Paraguay, Peru, Dominican Republic, Suriname, Uruguay, and Venezuela.

[130]http://www.corteidh.or.cr/index.php/es/acerca-de/como-acceder-al-sistema-interamericano/denuncias-consultas, Accessed on 23/10/2017.

The legal structure is formed, according to Fergus Mackay,[131] by two interrelated legal frameworks, the first constituted by (i) the 1948 Charter of the Organization of American States [OAS] and (ii) the American Declaration of the Rights and Duties of Man, which apply to all members of OAS, and the second group is composed of (i) the American Convention on Human Rights (Pact of San José, Costa Rica), and (ii) the Additional Protocol to the American Convention on Human Rights in the Area of Economic, Social and Cultural Rights (Protocol of San Salvador). To Mackay's list we can add (i) the United Nations Declaration on the Rights of Indigenous Peoples (General Assembly, 107th Plenary Session, 13 September 2007) and (ii) the American Declaration on the Rights of Indigenous Peoples (approved in the Dominican Republic in 2016).

The structure in charge of implementing the protection of human rights is made up of (i) the Inter-American Commission of Human Rights and (ii) the Inter-American Court of Human Rights. Each of them carries out their own functions that are not to be confused..

1 Inter-American Human Rights System

The following paragraphs contain an explanation of the main institutions that make up the Inter-American System of Human Rights, indicating their mandates and functions related to the theme of this work.

1.1 The Inter-American Commission on Human Rights

The Inter-American Commission on Human Rights is an organ of the Organization of American States, as established in Article 53 (e) of the charter by which it was created , with administrative powers aiming "to promote the observance and protection of human rights and to serve as a consultative organ of the Organization in these matters" (Article 106). According to the Pact of San José, Costa Rica, it is the

[131] MACKAY, Fergus. **A guide to indigenous peoples` rights in the Inter-American Human Rights System.** Copenhagen: IWGIA, 2002, p. 24.

responsibility of the Inter-American Commission on Human Rights, among other functions, "to take action on petitions and other communications pursuant to its authority under the provisions of Articles 44 through 51 of this Convention (Art. 41 f)." Access to the Inter-American Commission of Human Rights for the presentation of complaints is simplified, being widely facilitated to individuals, groups of individuals, or non-governmental organizations regularly constituted in according their countries' laws.

The work of the Inter-American Commission of Human Rights is structured around three points: (i) an Individual Petition System, (ii) monitoring of the human rights situation in Member States, and (iii) attention to the themes which have priority.[132]

The activities developed by the Commission are basically: (i) to receive, analyze, and investigate individual petitions that the Member States of the Organization of American States are confronted with, related to human rights violations, (ii) to monitor that Member States comply with human rights and, if deemed necessary, to publish information related to a certain State, (iii) to make *in loco* visits to the countries to check up on the local reality in relation to the matter of its attribution, and publish a report to be forwarded to the organs of the Organization of the American States, (iv) to promote awareness of human rights, (v) to recommend that Member States of the Organization of American States adopt measures that contribute to the protection of human rights in the countries of the continent, (vi) to request Member States to adopt precautionary measures, to prevent irreparable damage to people or to the object of a petition sent in severe and urgent cases. Such a measure can also be required of the Inter-American Court, (vii) to bring cases to the Inter-American Court, (viii) to consult with the Court according to Article 64 of the American Convention, and (ix) to receive and examine reports in which a Member State claims that another State committed human rights violations that are recognized in the American Convention.

[132] http://www.oas.org/pt/cidh/mandato/que.asp, Accessed on 23/10/2017.

1.2 Inter-American Court of Human Rights

The Inter-American Court of Human Rights is one of three regional courts dedicated to the protection of Human Rights,[133] the other two being the (i) European Court of Human Rights and (ii) the African Court of Human and Peoples' Rights. The antecedent of the Inter-American Court of Human Rights is the Ninth International Conference of American States, that took place in Bogota, Colombia, in 1948 when the States adopted the Resolution entitled 'Inter-American Court to Protect the Rights of Men'. The Inter-American Court was created by the American Convention on Human Rights, adopted in San José, Costa Rica, on 22 November 1969, and started its activities in 1979, one year after the Convention came into force. It is composed of seven national judges from the Member States of the Organization of American States, elected personally by the General Assembly of the international organ.

The Inter-American Court of Human Rights has two basic functions: one (i) a judicial function and the other (ii) an advisory function. The judicial function is that by which the Court determines the international responsibility of a State party to the Inter-American Convention on Human Rights for the violation of conventional provisions. The advisory function intends to provide the Member States with an interpretation of the Pact of San José (Costa Rica) and other international treaties on human rights that are recognized by the Inter-American Human Rights System.

The Inter-American Court of Human Rights, established by the Pact of San Jose in Costa Rica, is one of the organs with the competent knowledge of the issues related to the fulfillment of commitments assumed by the Member States regarding the Pact of San Jose, Article 33(b). Only the States Parties and the Commission shall have the right to submit a case to the Court, Article 61 (1), after all the procedures set forth in Articles 48 and 50 have been completed, that is, by the national legal bodies. If the Court finds that there has been a violation of a right

133 http://www.corteidh.or.cr/, Accessed on 23/10/2017.

or freedom protected by the Pact of San Jose, it is its responsibility to determine that the State adopts the necessary measures to remedy the violated right, or, when applicable, that adequate remedial measures be taken, including that fair compensation be paid to the injured party [Article 63(1)]. The decisions of the Court are final and not subject to appeal, however, the Court may interpret it at the request of any parties, provided the request is made within ninety days from the date of notification of the judgment. The decisions of the Inter-American Court of Human Rights are binding for the States that recognize its jurisdiction, and compensatory damages may be executed in the country from which the claim originated, in accordance with domestic procedure governing the execution of judgments against the state, 68 (1) and (2). As we will see next, the Court has played a very significant and active role in the matter.

The Inter-American Human Rights System has responded to the different issues presented by indigenous and traditional peoples related to the protection of human rights, by making the content of Free, Prior, and Informed Consent explicit in a very clear and indisputable way. It is important to note that both the Commission and the Court have converged towards definitions related to the topic, and moreover, the different national courts of countries in the hemisphere have similarly been facing the issues, making it evident that Free, Prior, and Informed Consent is a cogent and essential juridical reality for the legal use of natural resources that exist within indigenous territories and traditional communities. The decisions of the Court in relation to indigenous peoples and traditional populations have served as a standard for the decisions adopted by many national courts, defining the minimum content that should be observed by national jurisdictions.

1.2.1 Obligations of the States according to the Inter-American Court of Human Rights

The concrete content of the States' obligations *vis-à-vis* the Declarations of Human Rights and of indigenous peoples and Convention 169 concerning the effectiveness of the rights of indigenous and tribal peoples must be ascertained by the set of judicial and administrative decisions issued by the organs in charge of implementing the protective norms being used internationally, especially in the American hemisphere and its human rights protection system. From the large mass of decisions and cases it is possible to extract a synthesis of essential topics so that the current stage of legal evolution on the matter can be identified. A good guide for this task is the systemizing work[134] prepared by the Commission. This way we can identify the following standards of legal obligations to which the States of the Inter-American System for the Protection of Human Rights are subject, regarding the topic of free, prior, and informed consent.

a) The obligation to consult indigenous and tribal peoples and guarantee their participation in decisions and any measures that affect their territories must take into consideration the "special relationship of indigenous and tribal peoples with the land and natural resources', however, they do not only relate to issues of property rights.
b) The right to consultation and the state's duty to carry it out are linked to multiple human rights, particularly to Article 23 of the American Convention, as interpreted by the Court in the case YATAMA vs Nicaragua.[135] In the case of indigenous peoples, the right to participation in decision-making on matters of their interest must be exercised according to their institutions, values, uses, customs, and forms of organization.
c) In addition to the right to participation described in Article 23, the right of indigenous and tribal peoples to be consulted is fundamental for the realization of the rights to communal property of such communities.
d) The indigenous and tribal peoples' right to be consulted about decisions that may affect them is directly related to the right to cultural identity, inasmuch as their culture might be affected.

[134] http://cidh.org/countryrep/TierrasIndigenas2009/Cap.IX.htm#, Accessed on 23/10/2017.

[135] http://www.corteidh.or.cr/docs/casos/articulos/seriec_127_esp.pdf, Accessed on 09/10/2017.

e) Any administrative decision that might legally affect the rights and interests of indigenous and tribal peoples over their territories must be based on a process of full participation.

f) Every consultation process must seek consent without prejudice. The jurisprudence of the Court, in specific cases, and international standards demand that the States obtain the free and informed consent of indigenous peoples *prior to the execution* of plans and projects that may affect their property rights over lands, territory, and natural resources.

g) The Court highlights that the difference between 'consultation' and 'consent' entails that, when it comes to large-scale development and investment plans that have significant impact on indigenous and tribal territories, the State isn't only obliged to perform the consultation, but also to obtain free, prior, and informed consent from such populations, according to their traditions.[136]

h) The requirement of consent must be interpreted as a 'reinforced safeguard' for the rights of indigenous and tribal peoples, given its direct connection to the rights to life, cultural identity, and other essential human rights whenever development and investment plans affect the basic contents of such rights. "The duty to obtain consent corresponds, therefore, to a logic of proportionality between indigenous property rights and other associated rights".[137]

From the above list it is possible to conclude that states have the *obligation to consult* indigenous and tribal peoples and guarantee their participation in decision-making processes whenever there is an intention to take measures that may affect their territories. The way the consultation is carried out must be according to the uses, customs, traditions, and culture of the populations affected by the measures. Consent is required for decision-making regarding major development

[136] http://www.corteidh.or.cr/docs/casos/articulos/seriec_172_ing.pdf, Accessed on 09/10/2017.

[137] CIDH. **Derechos de los pueblos indígenas y tribales sobre sus tierras ancestrales y recursos naturales. Normas y jurisprudencia del Sistema Interamericano de Derechos Humanos**. December 2009, OEA/Ser.L/V/II. Doc. 56/09, paragraph. 333.

and investment projects that may affect indigenous and tribal territories. Nonetheless, it must be remarked that Inter-American jurisprudence admits that in exceptional circumstances, consent can be required as a measure of 'proportionality' between the forces at stake in relation to a specific enterprise.

1.2.2 The Jurisprudence of the Inter-American Court of Human Rights

The Court is extremely active in applying the different rules related to the Prior Consultation and Consent, whether they are covered in Convention 169 or defined in other international documents, always seeking to harmonize them in a single system of protection of human rights in the specific case of indigenous and tribal peoples.

Inter-American jurisprudence seeks to resolve some ambiguous aspects of Convention 169 because, even though the convention mentions the obligation to consult, when reading Articles 4, 6 and 7 it is possible to observe ambiguities in the adopted terms, since the 'consultation' has the objective of reaching an agreement that expresses the consent of indigenous and tribal peoples in relation to the intended intervention. On the other hand, these peoples are ensured the right to accept, or not, with measures for the environmental protection of their lands and others, as well as to define their own priorities. However, it would be naïve to believe that indigenous and tribal peoples have the right to veto the enterprises and projects designed to be implemented in their territories. The correlation of political forces simply makes the hypothesis unthinkable.

Convention 169 seeks to accommodate the interests at stake. Moreover, one can't overlook what is written in Article 34, which determines that "the nature and scope of the measures to be taken to give effect to this Convention shall be determined in a *flexible manner*, having regard to the conditions characteristic of each country." This way, there is a great margin for discretion whenever an insurmountable impasse appears. Therefore, it seems that the Convention 'gives with one hand and takes away with the other', leaving room for uncertainties.

However, as we will see further on in this work, it is possible to identify a growing international trend to try and 'reach an agreement and obtain consent'. Nonetheless, the critical point arises when the agreement doesn't seem to be possible, or the negotiations extend for too long.

1.2.2.1 Requirements for a Prior and Informed Consultation

To accomplish a Prior and Informed Consultation mechanism for indigenous and tribal peoples, valid in the eyes of the Court, the States must take into consideration that the Consultation must begin in the preliminary or planning stage of the intended activity, with reasonable anticipation, so that the affected group may understand the nature of the proposed intervention.

Understanding the nature of the intervention is a complex process that can be divided in at least three relevant points, being: (i) the language used to present the project to interested indigenous and tribal peoples, (ii) the demonstration of technical aspects of the enterprise in a simple manner, without, however, emptying it of its content, (iii) the positive and negative consequences, in relation to social, economic, cultural, and environmental aspects, that may arise from its implementation.

The Consultation must provide the community with the necessary elements to express its agreement or disagreement in a voluntary and informed way, which is consistent with Article 13 of the American Convention on Human Rights, with Article 19 (2) of the United Nations Declaration on the Rights of Indigenous Peoples, and with the American Declaration on the Rights of Indigenous Peoples.

The Consultation has a substantial character and is not to be mistaken for a mere bureaucratic or administrative formality.[138] It follows that the Consultation must be carried out in good faith and must seek to reach an *agreement* between the interested parties. Even

[138] Inter-American Court of Human Rights. Case of the Kichwa Indigenous People of Sarayaku vs. Ecuador. Sentence Serie C N° 245 of 27 June 2012 (Fund and Reparations). Available at: http://www.corteidh.or.cr/docs/ casos/articulos/seriec_245_esp.pdf, Accessed on 09/10/2017.

though there is no formal definition of the concept of good faith, it is an objective concept that can be identified on a case-by-case basis and that excludes the practice of coercion of indigenous communities, requires trust and loyalty in the presentation of the issues, the absence of cooptation and corruption of local leaderships and all other things that may undermine the social cohesion of the indigenous or tribal community involved in the consultation process. As a natural consequence of such determinations, States must provide for the creation of legal, political, and administrative instruments and mechanisms that are able to ensure that the decision-making process is at a qualified level of information for the indigenous and tribal peoples.[139] In all cases, the consultation must make use of mechanisms traditionally used by indigenous peoples to deliberate, that is, it must be culturally appropriate, which concretely means the use of their own mechanisms, such as customs and traditions of indigenous and tribal peoples to verify results. This interpretation is consistent with Article 15 of Convention 169 and with Article 32 (2) of the United Nations Declaration on the Rights of Indigenous Peoples, Art. XIII (2). Finally, it must be stated that the corroboration of the legitimacy of the representation of indigenous and tribal peoples must be done according to the customs and traditions of the indigenous and tribal peoples concerned.

1.2.3 Consultation, Agreement, and Consent

This is perhaps the most sensitive point regarding the participation of indigenous and tribal peoples in matters related to the different types of projects and enterprises that may affect their modes of living, traditions, culture, and impact their territory. Article 6 of Convention

[139] Inter-American Court of Human Rights. Case of the Saramaka People v. Suriname. Sentence of 28 November 2007 (Preliminary Objections, Merit, Reparations, and Costs), in, Jurisprudence of the Inter-American Court of Human Rights / National Bureau of Justice, Commission of Amnesty, Inter-American Court of Human Rights. Portuguese Translation of the Inter-American Court of Human Rights. Brasilia: Ministry of Justice, 2014. p. 286.

169 states that when applying their provisions, governments must *consult* the peoples concerned. As for Article 6 (2), it establishes that 'the consultations carried out in application of this Convention shall be undertaken, in good faith and in a form appropriate to the circumstances, with the objective of achieving agreement or consent to the proposed measures.' Therefore, it seems clear that Consultation is not an end in itself, rather, a mechanism for obtaining the opinion of the community involved about the intended project or activity by third parties in their territories.

As it is known, an agreement is the manifestation of a common will between two or more parties about a certain issue. First, we must recall that the Vienna Convention on the Law of Treaties, which was incorporated into Brazilian Law by Decree no. 7030 of 14 December 2009, in Article 26 establishes that 'every treaty in force is binding upon the parties to it and must be performed by them in good faith.' Therefore, it seems reasonable that the agreement described in Article 6 (2) of Convention 169 can only be interpreted as consent, as it is hard to imagine the hypothesis in which a consultation carried out according to the standards established by the pertinent International Conventions and implemented by the standards defined by the Inter-American Court of Human Rights can result in an agreement *that does not express the agreement (rectius: consent)* of the indigenous and tribal peoples concerned, regarding a measure being planned or implemented.

However, in the aforementioned Saramaka case, the Court considered the possibility of differences between Consultation and Consent because it perceived that such hypotheses "require further analysis". It should be noted that the Court expresses the understanding that the level of Consultation required in each case shall vary according to the degree of intervention considered by the project, and is therefore flexible.

> Furthermore, it considers that in addition to the required consultation, whenever a development or investment project inside the traditional Saramaka territory is presented, the guarantee of effective participation required in the case of large development or investment projects that may have a profound impact on the

> property rights of the Saramaka people in much of their territory, it must be understood as an additional requirement to the obligation of obtaining free, prior, and informed consent of the Saramaka people, according to their customs and traditions.[140]

The question is: in the case of less significant impact, is intervention allowed even if no agreement is reached? Here, it seems evident that extremely relevant issues are at stake, and they must remain points for reflection.

First there is the problem - always present - of relations between ethnic minorities and the national community. To what extent can an ethnic minority stop the realization of projects that are *proven* to bring benefits to a larger community and, on the other hand, if the wider community is granted rights in the name of their benefits, this can create disproportionate burdens on the minority community. For the sake of argumentFor the sake of argument, the limit is set at the concrete threat to the physical, ethnic, and cultural survival of that community, taking into consideration the concrete or potential impact to be produced by the proposed activity.

It is important to consider that Article 34 of Convention 169 establishes that the measures to be adopted to provide efficacy to the terms of the Convention must be flexible and according to the reality of each country. Therefore, it's necessary to consider the dimension of the project to be implemented in relation to the total economy of the host country and, obviously, the degree of impact upon indigenous and tribal territories. As an operational criterion it seems reasonable that a benefit for the national society cannot result in excessive and disproportionate

140 "Similarly, in Maya Indigenous Communities of the Toledo District v. Belize, the Inter-American Commission observed that States must undertake effective and fully informed consultations with indigenous communities with regard to acts or decisions that may affect their traditional territories. In said case, the Commission determined that a process of "fully informed consent" requires "at a minimum, that all of the members of the community are fully and accurately informed of the nature and consequences of the process and provided with an effective opportunity to participate individually or as collectives". Cf. Inter-American Commission on Human Rights, Report 40/04, Merit. Case 12.052. Mayan Indigenous Communities in the District of Toledo, note 84 supra, par. 142. Cf. also The Equator Principles, Principle 5."

negative burdens to the indigenous and tribal peoples and, conversely, a benefit to indigenous and tribal peoples cannot result in disproportionate losses to national society. These criteria, it seems, are still extremely subjective, and the answers to the controversy must be sought in the positive norms.

CHAPTER 7

Prior consultation before the Courts of South America

1 – Introduction

The Constitutional Courts of South America, as well as the lower courts, have been debating the issues related to Prior Consultation and Consent stipulated by Convention 169 with great frequency since the end of the twentieth century.[141] We can affirm that all South American nations have discussed the issue in court and, as we will see, the decisions issued by the Inter-American Court of Human Rights have served as a decision standard for national courts. Evidently, there are greater and lesser degrees of compliance with the Inter-American Court's sentences.

2 Judicial decisions by South American Courts

2.1 Argentina

Although Argentina doesn't have a very vast jurisprudence on the subject of the application of Convention 169, it has accumulated a few decisions of the Supreme Court of Justice of the Nation, which, for the most part, don't confront the merit of the issue and are limited to determining that the lower Courts reassess the matter according to the cogent constitutional legal devices. It should likewise be noted that the

[141] For a broad overview of the case. ILO. **La aplicación del convenio núm. 169 por tribunales nacionales e internacionales en américa Latina: una compilación de casos / organización internacional del trabajo**. Geneva ILO, 2009, passim.

federative structure of the country prevents many of the issues from reaching the Supreme Court, for its competences are expressed and, in a certain way, limited. Procedures appear before local courts and don't always reach the Supreme Court. Some selected cases will be presented next.

2.1.1 The Quompi-Lqataxac Nam Qompi Case

In 2006, the Chamber of Contentious-Administrative Jurisdiction of the *Chaco* province granted a protective measure – a procedure similar to the Brazilian Security Warrant – required by the *Quompi-Lqataxac Nam Qompi* council before the *Chaco* Province, whose object was:

(I) obtaining a register of indigenous communities and organizations in the Province, according to Article 37 of the provincial Constitution and Article 75, 17 of the National Constitution and ILO Convention 169;

(II) declaring Law no. 4.804 which created the Record of Indigenous Communities and Organizations unconstitutional, since the discussion and elaboration of said legal norm was not preceded with the necessary free, prior, and informed Consultation with indigenous communities and organizations and, also,

(III) declaring Articles 5 and 6 of Law no. 3258 unconstitutional (this rule is prior to the coming into force of the constitutional reform of 1994), since these articles violated indigenous rights recognized by both the *Chaco* Province Constitution and by Article 5 of Convention 169.

The controversy stemmed from the refusal of the provincial authority to recognize the juridical entity of the *Lqataxac Nam Qompi* community, compromising their ability to obtain financing and funds to build a school for the community. In their defense, the Chaco Province pleaded the rejection of the claim by arguing that it was a matter of administrative contentious jurisdiction and, furthermore, that after the constitutional reform of 1994 there were legal changes and alterations in the applicable legal framework, and also that the parties had not reached a consensus for the regulation of the topic. It was added that the recognition of indigenous communities had a constitutive, not a merely declaratory, character. Therefore, it was necessary that indigenous communities met certain legal requirements so that they could be recognized by the administrative authority as worthy of special protection.

During the procedural instruction it was fully demonstrated that, effectively, during the period of processing the bill that led to Law 4804/00, there was absolutely no consultation made with the indigenous peoples concerned. The court recognized that the 'usual practice' of most legislators was to forgo the summoning of interested parties in the case of legislating for indigenous peoples, thus forgetting the mandatory participation imposed by the Constitution.

The Court also determined that the participation mandated by both the National and the Provincial Constitution means that indigenous peoples must take part in the processes of developing, executing, and controlling decisions related to any future actions taken by the State – even those delegated to private parties – in indigenous territories and/or their area of influence, or that are directly or indirectly related to the affected people.

Finally, the Court found section c) of Article 2 of Law no. 4804 to be unconstitutional, for it was approved without prior consultation with indigenous peoples, in violation of Articles 37 and 75, section 17, of the Constitution of the *Chaco* Province.

2.1.2 The Crecencio Pilquiman Case against the Autonomous Institute of Colonization and Rural Development [Instituto Autárquico de Colonización y Fomento Rural]. Protective action[142]

The matter was submitted to the Judiciary through a protective claim proposed by Crecencio Pilquiman[143] and his wife before the Institute

[142] Sentence. October 7, 2014 Supreme Court of Justice of the Nation. Federal Capital, Autonomous City of Buenos Aires. Magistrates: Lorenzetti, Faytt, Highton, Maqueda, Zaffaronild SAIJ: FA14000148, in, http://www.saij.gob.ar/corte-suprema-justicia-nacion-federal-ciudad-autonoma-buenos-aires-pilquiman-crecencio-instituto-autarquico-colonizacion-fom e nto-rural-accion-amparo-fa14000148-2014-10-07/123456789-841-0004-1ots-eupmocsollaf?,Accessed on 12/07/2017.

[143] http://infojusnoticias.gov.ar/opinion/la-corte-suprema-y-el-derecho-a-la-consulta-de-los-pueblos-indigenas-144.html, Accessed on 11/07/2017.

of Colonization and Rural Development [*Instituto Autárquico de Colonización y Fomento Rural*], aiming to ensure the right of the indigenous communities *Lagunita Salada, Gorro Frigio and Cerro Bayo* (*Mapuche* ethnicity), of which he is a member, to participate in matters related to their territory and the use of its natural resources. Twenty-five thousand hectares of public land – in a site next to the aforementioned community, which contains an indigenous cemetery –, was handed over to a local farmer, even though, according to the plaintiff, that territory belonged to the indigenous community. The claim was judged unfounded by the court of origin (Chubut Province), thus confirming the action of the Institute.

El abogado del Instituto de Colonización, Dr. Bezunartea, defendió la actuación del organismo, y afirmó que el IAC no tenía por qué consultar a la Comunidad antes de reconocerle derechos sobre el predio en discusión a Rechene.

The plaintiff based his appeal on Article 75, section 17 of the National Constitution and on Convention 169, having obtained a provisional remedy to stop the assignment of the lands. The decision was reversed in favour of the farmer in the Family Court of *Puerto Madryn*, in the Chamber of Appeals, and even in the Superior Court of Justice of Chubut. One of the main arguments used to deny the Pilquimans' claim was the assertion that the *Mapuches* are not Argentinian, because they would have come from Chile after the country's founding.

Refusing to accept the unfavourable decisions, the *Pilquimans* lodged an appeal appeal before the Supreme Court of Justice, which annulled the precious decision, considering the decisions of the lower instances to be arbitrary, which is why they should be annulled. The Supreme Court understood that the lower courts had become attached to excessive formalities with an "unjustified formal rigour" that led to a "frustration of rights", especially that of the constitutional guarantee of a full defense in court. As a result, the constitutional court determined that the files be sent back to the ordinary instances, for a new judgment with due regard for constitutional guarantees.

2.2 Bolivia

2.2.1 Hydrocarbon Law

Bolivia is known to be a great producer of natural gas, the vast majority of which is exported to Brazil through a gas pipeline named Gasbol. The Bolivian section of Gasbol starts in Rio Grande, a small village with only 400 inhabitants of indigenous origin, and it extends 557 km to Porto Suarez, on the border with Brazil.[144] The activity is of great importance for the Andean country and, evidently, has repercussions on the original peasant populations of that Andean nation.

The Bolivian Plurinational Constitutional Court, through Constitutional Sentence 0045/2006,[145] had the opportunity to examine the constitutionality of Articles 114 and 115, among others, of the Hydrocarbon Law (17 May 2005) that deal with the consultation and participation of originary peoples when handling the use of natural resources in indigenous territories. In this specific case, the Plurinational Constitutional Court examined a direct appeal for unconstitutionality filed by a deputy who thought the above mentioned articles to be unconstitutional. The reasons for the unconstitutionality resided in the fact that, according to the congressman, articles attributed to indigenous peoples' rights were not granted to other sectors of the Bolivian society, thus violating isonomy among citizens.

The Plurinational Constitutional Court found that the disputed norms were the result of compliance with Articles 4, 6, 15, and 18 of Convention 169 of the International Labour Organization. In the Court's view, these articles are part of the 'constitutionality set', that is, they must be understood as constitutional norms.

The Plurinational Constitutional Court is based on the reasoning that Article 15 (b) of Convention 169 imposes the need for consultation, but doesn't establish that the agreement with indigenous

[144] http://www.tbg.com.br/pt_br/o-gasoduto/tracado.htm, Accessed on 29/10/2017.
[145] https://jurisprudencia.tcpbolivia.bo/, Accessed on 29/10/2017.

peoples is a necessary requirement for the execution of works. The Bolivian court found that the objective of the consultation, in the specific case, is to quantify the damage that indigenous and tribal peoples may suffer as a result of the planned activity, and it concluded that prior, mandatory, and timely consultation is compatible with the Bolivian Constitution and Convention 169. The court concluded that indigenous communities don't have the right of veto over enterprises in the case of Article 15 (2) of Convention 169.[146] Finally, the Court remarks that the Hydrocarbon Law ensures the payment of an equitable compensation to the indigenous peoples, so they are not left unprotected. In conclusion, the Court declares the obligation to consult with indigenous peoples and the binding quality of the consultation's results as unconstitutional.[147]

[146] "'In conclusion, the provision under consideration (Article 15.2 of ILO Convention No. 169) imposes an obligation on the State to carry out consultation on the effects on the interests of the indigenous and tribal peoples, taking into account the specific sociological situation of the relevant peoples; such consultation does not have a determining or definitive character in terms of requiring the agreement of these peoples in order to be able exploit the sub-surface resources that are the property of the State, but rather, the provision under consideration imposes the duty to consult whether these interests may be harmed so that the peoples may be duly and fairly indemnified. Therefore, consultation is not to be understood as a request for authorisation, but rather, implies an effective consultation with the indigenous and tribal peoples who occupy the territories that are the object of the exploitation, regarding the quantification of harm to their interests that may be suffered as an effect of the extraction, and of course, cannot be seen as the power to prevent the exploitation of the sub-surface resources that belong to the State, since the overriding interests of the majority as expressed by the State authorities are above the interests of any type of group".

[147] "With respect to what is disposed by the rules of Art. 115 of the HL, it must be stated that its text reflects the Hydrocarbon Law's adoption of the right of consultation established by Art. 15.2 of ILO Convention 169; however, when establishing that said consultation aims at not only determining how the interests of indigenous and peasant peoples are affected, but also at obtaining their consent, it dismisses what is disposed by the constitutionality blockade, since as was already analyzed, the aforementioned Art. 15.2 of the ILO Convention doesn't have this purpose, especially when, as already stated, the hydrocarbons are property of the State; therefore, no person, part of a group or group of people can oppose the exploitation of hydrocarbon riches, which doesn't imply that the affected groups of said explorations are deprived of their rights, since as a result of the consultation about the effects they will suffer, they should receive fair compensation, which must be established on a case by case basis, according to Art. 116 of the HL. The application

2.2.2 Isiboro Sécure Indigenous Territory and National Park (TIPNIS)

An important Bolivian judicial decision on the subject is Plurinational Constitutional Sentence 0300/2012, founding sentence,[148] which established the parameters to be followed for the application of the Consultation. The case was about an unconstitutionality claim of Law 222 (Law of consultation with the indigenous peoples of the Isiboro Sécure Indigenous Territory and National Park - TIPNIS).[149] The Bolivian government planned to build a road (*Villa Tunari – San Ignacio de Moxos*) passing through the TIPNIS. Due to pressures against the construction of the road, the government sanctioned Law 180 of October 2011, which declared the territory to be intangible and prohibited the construction of the road. However, soon afterwards, Law 222 of February 2012 on Prior Consultation was promulgated, for the continuity of road construction through the TIPNIS. The judgement commented on here is related to the constitutionality of Law 222. The basis for the unconstitutionality claim of the law resided in the fact that it could not be applied to the TIPNIS issue, because it was put into effect after the beginning of the construction works on the road.

of Convention 169 by national and international courts in Latin America, on the other hand, with regard to the compulsory nature of the consultation, stated that the rule can have two meanings, one being constitutional and the other not; thus, the first of them imposes the inescapable duty to consult indigenous peoples about the harm they may suffer due to hydrocarbon activity, according to the supralegal rule; nevertheless, the provisions of Art. 115 of the HL, in giving a mandatory value to the result of the consultation as an authorization, is a secondary understanding of obligation, aimed at granting authority to the consultation and a binding value to the State, the consent of the indigenous people to develop the hydrocarbon activity, which exceeds the provisions of the constitutional blockade, which, as previously stated, is not intended to stopis not intended to stop the exploitation of sub-surface resources belonging to the State; therefore, this obligation must be understood in the sense that consultation is an inescapable duty of the State; hence the sentence: 'to obtain obtain consent from the communities and indigenous and originary peoples' is unconstitutional, and must be so declared".

[148] Court decisions that establish a new understanding on a certain matter.

[149]http://www.oeco.org.br/reportagens/25872-estrada-pelo-tipnis-a-novela-continua/, Accessed on 10/10/2017.

Upon deciding on the matter, the Plurinational Constitutional Court[150] found that consultation, at first, should precede the implementation of the project, plan, or measure that is affecting the rights of indigenous peoples, or take place before the approval of the law or any other normative action that may affect them. In the decision, the Court made an express reference to the decisions professed by the Commission and by the Inter-American Court of Human Rights, highlighting that consultation must precede construction work and begin during the planning stages. To support the argument, the Plurinational Constitutional Court stated that:

> Likewise, in its resolution on the Saramaka case, the Inter-American Court pointed out that consultation with indigenous peoples must be made during the early stages of a development or investment plan or mining concession project, and 'not only when the need arises to obtain approval of the community, if such is the case. arly notice provides time for proper feedback to the State..." (Inter-American Court of Human Rights. Case of the Saramaka People v. Suriname. Preliminary Objections, Merit, Reparations, and Costs. Sentence of 28 November 2007. Series C, N. 172 , par. 133) .

The Court found that, according to Article 32.2 of the Declaration on the Rights of Indigenous Peoples, consultation must be prior and, therefore, prior to the approval of any project that affects their lands or territories and resources. The Court added that if the consultation is not prior "there is indeed a reduction in the rights of indigenous peoples". The violation can be combated through its own constitutional actions, as ensured by signed precedent SC 1018/2011-R, of 22 June, from a systematic interpretation of Article 135 of the Political Constitution of the State. However, when facing the specific case, the Plurinational Constitutional Court found that:

> However, it must be clarified that when the initial omission is resolved and, for example, the consultation goes ahead and is carried out, or a law on it is issued in accordance with the Constitution and

[150] http://ajurisprudencia.tcpbolivia.bo/jurisprudencia/envio/enviocontenido.php?fnombres=consulta%20previa&tiposentencia=0&tiporecurso=0, Accessed on 10/10/2017.

> the international rules on human rights, this rule cannot be considered unconstitutional or contrary to the constitutionality blockade because, even though it is not prior and for this reason there was – as mentioned – harm to indigenous peoples' rights; this rule is, however, complying to a collective right, albeit belatedly.
>
> To understand it otherwise would imply that the harm caused to indigenous people's rights can't be repaired under any circumstance. Because, in claiming that the Consultation was not prior, the laws issued for that purpose would have to be deemed unconstitutional, which would lead us to the absurdity of maintaining a state of unconstitutional affairs for an undetermined time, a situation that is neither allowed nor desired by the constitutional order, nor by norms in international treaties on human rights.

Based on the aforementioned reasoning, the Bolivian Court admitted that in cases in which projects had initiated without Prior Consultation, it is possible to try to accomodate the positions in a way that does not invalidate or annul already initiated procedures. The Court understands that, although the ideal is that the consult be made before the decision-making, if that doesn't occur, however, the obligation of consulting "does not disappear, in fact, consultation is even more necessary, because there would in fact be a violation, of the rights of indigenous peoples over their territory and of the right to consultation itself". The Plurinational Constitutional Court assumes that the adopted position is in line with international jurisprudence on the matter that determines that the Consultation is carried out even if the projects are being implemented, since otherwise it could be wrongly concluded that an already implemented project would have the power to nullify the right of indigenous and tribal peoples to Consultation.

> With this understanding it is concluded that Art. 1° of Law i 222, on the summoning of free informed consultation doesn't contradict constitutional provisions, nor constitutional blockade rules; according to what is reiterated, it allows for peoples to exercise their right regarding the measures that directly affect them and that, therefore, there is compliance with the provisions in Arts . 30.II.15 of CPE, 6.1 of [Convention 169 of] OIT and 19 of the Declaration [of the United Nations] on the Rights of Indigenous Peoples.

> A contrary understanding, in the sense noted by the plaintiffs, that is, that Law 222 is unconstitutional because it was not preceded by legal and administrative actions, which began in 2006, would imply that the harm to indigenous peoples' rights could not be repaired under any circumstance or hypothesis; thus leading to the absurdity of maintaining the unconstitutional omission indefinitely, and this is not the purpose of the State's Political Constitution, nor of Convention 169, nor the United Nations Declaration on the Rights of Indigenous Peoples, nor the jurisprudence of the Inter-American Court of Human Rights, as was extensively discussed in the legal basis III.4.1 of this decision .

It is indeed a pragmatic decision since, from a practical point of view, the unconstitutionality declaration of Law 222 would in no way improve the situation of the indigenous people regarding the construction of the road, which was, as seems so obvious, a fait accompli. Here too, we must observe that the mere declaration of intangibility of the park (Law 180) was absolutely inefficient, because the administration made use of a very common stratagem in similar cases: construction begins on opposite sides and the protected area is located 'in the middle' of the road, generating a fait accompli.

2.3 Chile

The Chilean Judiciary Branch, through the Supreme Court Directorate of Studies,[151] organized the jurisprudencial tendencies of the high court regarding the rights of indigenous peoples, especially in relation to Convention 169 and Free, Prior Informed Consultation. Much of the identified jurisprudencial tendencies are linked to the interseccion of indigenous and environmental issues, above all regarding the use of natural resources.

The Chilean Supreme Court understands that Article 6 (1) of Convention 169 establishes that Consultation with the people concerned aims to uphold an agreement regarding the proposed measures that might affect indigenous territories or impact their

[151] http://decs.pjud.cl/index.php/tendencias, Accessed on 04/06/2017.

traditional lifestyles, however, " form of participation could never constitute a binding popular consultation or affect the privative attributions of the authorities that are determined by the Fundamental Charter'. According to the Court, Article 5 of the Chilean Constitution establishes that sovereignty essentially resides in the Nation, and is exercised through periodic referenda and elections, as well as by the authorities defined in the Constitution itself, thus signaling that no sector of the people, nor any individual, can assign themselves to such an exercise. Therefore, just like all other inhabitants of the country, indigenous peoples are subject to the constitutional order in force, "without the transfer of power which, in fact, implies an exercise of sovereignty". Finally, the Court finds that the consultative participation treated by Convention 169 does not imply that indigenous peoples are attributed with "powers or public authorities, but rather consolidates the right that assists them in being consulted in the matters that concern them (C.S., 14/10/2010, Rol: 4078-10)."

With regard to indigenous participation in environmental licensing processes for projects that may affect their territories, it is understood that it is mandatory when such processes of environmental licensing are carried out due to the requirement of prior studies on environmental impact. However, the Court understands that the determination of the existence, or not, of the impact on an indigenous community must be done in accordance with national legislation (Law 19.300, Law on General Environmental Bases[152]) (autos rol 2211-2012, of 27/4/2012; 10090-2011, of 22/3/2012; 11040-2011, of 30/3/2012; 258-2011, of 13/7/2011; 6062-2010, of 4/1/2011). Ergo, there is no fundamental difference between consultation as stipulated by specific environmental legislation and consultation as specified in Convention 169:

> The procedure of citizen participation in the projects submitted to an environmental impact study – determined in Article 26 of Law no. 19.300 – is the mechanism that leads to mandatory consultation according to Convention 169, whose text and principles are fully

[152] https://www.leychile.cl/Navegar?idNorma=30667, Accessed on 06/06/2017.

compatible and achieve efficacy with the current environmental regulation (C.S. 14/10/2010, Rol: 4078-2010)."

Considering the determination of Convention 169 regarding Prior Consultation in planning and preliminary stages of projects, the Court finds that at the stage of requesting concessions for the exploitation of geothermal energy on indigenous territories, it is not applicable to hold this hearing, just as the Consultation is not applicable in cases of grant concessions for the touristic exploitation of protected areas (Court of Appeals of Santiago, Rol 12.533-12, of 16 November 2012, deliberation 9 (refuted). Sentence confirmed by Supreme Court, Rol 9527-12, of 17 January 2013).

The decisions of the Supreme Court regarding the application of Convention 169 have been strongly criticized by the specialized doctrine, and it has also criticized the Chilean regulation of the matter through Supreme Decree 124 of 4 September 2009,[153] especially in Articles 3, 4 and 5. According to the specialized doctrine.[154] What supports this criticism is that Decree 124 reduced the scope of the terms of Convention 169, and it actually denies consultations with indigenous peoples, because when it refers the Consultation to sectoral rules, it forgets that the main Chilean sectoral rules - on mining, water, electricity - contains no legal provision on consultation. This only happens with the Law on the General Basis of the Environment , which stipulates a general regime of public consultation without any particular concern for indigenous peoples.

[153] https://www.leychile.cl/Navegar?idNorma=1006486, Accessed on 31/10/2017.

[154] CONTESSE, Jorge and LOVERA, Domingo. **El Convenio 169 de la OIT en la jurisprudencia chilena: prólogo del incumplimiento**, in, Anuario de Derecho Público 2011, Santiago: Universidad Diego Portales.

2.4 Colombia

The Constitutional Court of Colombia has ruled on countless issues related to the implementation of Convention 169, with special emphasis on matters related to the issues of Prior Consultation and consent of indigenous and tribal peoples to interventions that may affect their territories and ways of life.

2.4.1 Exploitation of Natural Resources in Indigenous Territories

The SU-039/97 sentence issued by the Constitutional Court of Colombia[155] was the result of a protective action presented by the Ombudsman in favour of the U`wa indigenous people and before the Ministry of the Environment. The Ombudsman claimed that the indigenous peoples' right to a full consultation regarding the exploitation of hydrocarbons in their territories had been denied, since a simple meeting with community leaders doesn't suffice as a process of Free, Prior and Informed Consultation. For this reason, he requested the annulment of the granted environmental license,due to the violation of Articles 6 and 15 of Convention 169. The company responsible for the activity argued that it had complied with all legal procedures and that it had also held about 33 meetings with the communities in question, and that the meetings were not merely formalities, as was alleged by the Ombudsman.

In reaching a decision, the Constitutional Court found that:

> The exploitation of natural resources in indigenous territories must be compatible with the protection the State must provide to the social, cultural, and economical integrity of indigenous communities. This integrity constitutes a fundamental right for the community, because it is linked to their subsistence as a human group and as a culture. To assure this integrity, when it comes to the exploitation of natural resources in indigenous territories, the participation of the community in the decisions taken to authorize

[155] http://www.corteconstitucional.gov.co/relatoria/1997/su039-97.htm, Accessed on 02/11/2017.

> said exploitation was determined. Therefore, the community's fundamental right of preserving integrity is guaranteed and carried out through the exercise of another right, which is also fundamental, the community's right to participate in decision making. The participation of indigenous communities in the decisions that may affect them regarding the exploitation of natural resources offers the particularity that the aforementioned participation, through the Consultation mechanism, acquires the connotation of a fundamental right, since it is built as a basic instrument to preserve ethnic, social, economic, and cultural integrity of indigenous communities, thus ensuring their survival as a social group. In this way, participation is not reduced to a mere intervention in administrative action aimed at guaranteeing the right of defense of those affected by the authorization of the environmental license, but it has a greater meaning due to the high interests it seeks to protect, as well as those related to the definition of destiny and safety of the subsistence of the above-mentioned communities.

The Constitutional Court, based on Articles 40 and 330 of the Colombian Constitution and with the rules of Convention 169. According to the understanding of the Constitutional Court, consultation with communities that may be affected by the exploitation of natural resources requires the adoption of communication measures and understandings characterized by mutual respect and good faith between the concerned parties, with the purpose of achieving:

(i) that the community has full knowledge of projects designed to exploit natural resources in the territories they occupy or own, and of the required mechanisms, procedures, and activities to carry them out;

(ii) that the community be informed about the way in which the execution may involve a disregard for the elements that constitute the basis of their cultural, social, economic, and political cohesion and, finally, their subsistence as a human group with unique characteristics;

(iii) that the opportunity is given so the community can, freely and without external interferences, by summoning its members, evaluate the advantages and disadvantages that the project will bring to the community and that their evaluation is heard, so that their concerns and expectations, regarding the defense of their interests, be presented to the authorities and the entrepreneurs with their implications.

The Court established that, in the event that an agreement with the community is not possible,

> "...the decision of the authority must be devoid of arbitrariness or authoritarianism; consequently it must be objective, reasonable, and proportional to the constitutional purpose that requires the State to protect the social, cultural, and economic identity of the indigenous community".

In addition, the Constitutional Court determined that mechanisms capable of mitigating, correcting, or restoring the effects authority measures may produce to the detriment of the community or its members must be arbitrated. The court concluded:

> "Therefore, the information or notification offered to the indigenous community about a project for the exploitation of natural resources has no value as Consultation. It is necessary to comply with the aforementioned directives, to present the agreement or arrangements with the community, and finally, that the community expresses, through authorized representatives, its conformity or nonconformity with said project and the way it affects their ethnic, cultural, social, and economic identity.

2.4.2 The Rural Development Statute [EDR]

The case regarding the constitutionality of the Rural Development Statute [Estatuto do Desenvolvimento Rural (EDR)] is very relevant, as it concerns the right to consultation and participation in the legislative process in the event that the bill is able to have an impact on the territories of indigenous and tribal peoples.

Sentence C- 175/09[156] was declared in an unconstitutionality claim of EDR owing to the omission of the state duty of Prior Consultation with indigenous communities and other ethnic groups that could be affected by the rule. The authors of the legal measure contested Law 1.152/07 in its entirety, on the grounds of violation of Articles 2, 7, 40, and 330 of the Colombian Constitution and Article 6 of ILO Convention 169, because indigenous and Afro-descendant communities were not consulted at the time of drafting the bill, nor during the proceedings before Congress. The authors reported that during the processing of the bill, some informative meetings for some social sectors had taken place, which were, however, not sufficient to attend to the determinations of Sentence SU - 039/97 of the Constitutional Court, therefore, they did not comply with the requirements for the consultation to be considered legally valid.

According to the impugnation, ILO Convention 169 establishes that governments have the obligation to respect the fact that the connection to land and territories is important to the culture and the spiritual values of indigenous and tribal peoples, which is dealt with in various articles of the Convention itself. In this specific case, the EDR has many dispositions related to indigenous and tribal peoples, so it has unequivocal repercussions on those communities. Despite these considerations, the affected communities could not exercise their right to Prior Consultation, a fact that contaminates the entire EDR, which is why they required an unconstitutionality declaration for the entire Law 1152/07.

The Constitutional Court understood that Law 1.152/07 is a "comprehensive and systematic regulation on rural development and the use and utilization of rural property" and as such must be submitted to the process of Prior Consultation with indigenous and Afro-descendant communities "due to the special connotation that the territory has for these peoples". It also added that the process of clarification and consultation developed by the government with the

[156] http://www.corteconstitucional.gov.co/relatoria/2009/C-175-09.htm, Accessed on 02/06/2017.

indigenous and Afro-descendent communities was not adequate, because it was initiated when the legal proceedings of the bill were already at an advanced stage, which indicated a 'circumstance incompatible with the validity of the good faith principle in the processes of Prior Consultation', impeding any validation of what had already been done by the administration.

The consultations formulated by the Administration could be seen as the expression of a general right to participate, which cannot be mistaken with

> ...the concrete modalities of indigenous and Afro-descendant communities referred to in Article 6 of ILO Convention 169, which correspond to a substantive procedure of a constitutional nature, aimed at satisfying the fundamental right to Prior Consultation that indigenous and Afro-descendant communities are entitled to.

In view of the above mentioned issues, the Court understood that the entire rule must be judged unconstitutional, with the decision having effects for the future.

2.4.3 Cartagena – Beach

With Sentence T-376/12,[157] the Constitutional Court dealt with the tutelage request[158] presented by Jovannys Pardo Castro before the Maritime Directorate of the Port Authority of the Tourist and Cultural District of Cartagena, on the basis that the authority violated her fundamental rights, at least of subsistence, of labour, of the due legal process, and also violated the principle of legitimate trust, as well as the fundamental right of the Communitary Councils of the Afro-descendant community of the Communitary Unit Rural Government of La Boquilla, Parish of Virgin Mary, and of the Tourist and Cultural District of Cartagena, since she was not consulted prior to the concession of an area of 8194 m^2 of beach in the region of Cielo Mar La Boquilla (Cartagena) to the company Talarame Inversiones y

[157] http://www.corteconstitucional.gov.co/relatoria/2012/T-376-12.htm, Accessed on 02/06/2017.
[158] See note 47.

Compania SA. According to the allegations of the plaintiff, she worked on the beach, in the tourist sector, for fifteen years, and on 5 July 2011 she was prevented from working by the administration of the Torre de las Americas Building, using the argument that the latter had rights to make use of the beach because of a permit issued by the Maritime Directorate of the Port Authority of Cartagena. The plaintiff claimed, in addition, that the inhabitants of La Boquilla are organized as a Community Council - according Law 70 of 1993 - so they are supported by ILO Convention 169, which establishes that it is mandatory to consult indigenous and Afro-descendant communities before adopting measures that may affect their interests. The plaintiff pointed out that Resolution 0497/2099 of the Port Authority granted concession to the Talamare Company of a beach area equivalent to 8195 m^2 without consulting the community of La Boquilla, in contradiction with ILO Convention 169, in particular with Articles 6 and 7, and with constitutional jurisprudence.

When deciding on the specific case, the Colombian Court found that:

> The right to participation of ethnically distinctive communities is realized in three levels of participation, of different intensities: (i) 'simple participation' in the face of measures that assume an indirect and only accidental interest to the community; (ii) Prior Consultation regarding measures that affect them directly; and (iii) Free, Prior, and Informed Consent regarding those that involve an especially intense affect, as defined by constitutional jurisprudence'

The jurisprudence of the Court (sentences T - 244/2012 and T 348/2012) recognized the right to direct participation of vulnerable people and human groups in urban projects and macro-projects aimed at restoring the Barzuto Market and the construction of roads. By analyzing previous cases, the understanding was established that the exclusion of participation of vulnerable groups in urban projects and the decisions associated with them, constitute a violation of the right of participation, which "usually results in threats or violations of other rights because the absence of participation leads to decision-making that does not attend to all constitutionally relevant aspects." It is important to observe that in the precedents, the Court, through its Seventh Chamber, determined that meetings should be held to "reach an agreement on the appropriate compensation and relocation measures for the affected, taking into account that, in part, the claimants were not indigenous or Afro-descendant communities, entitled to the right to Prior Consultation...". In this case, the plaintiff party was the black community of La Boquilla which held the right, having demonstrated that the disputed measure had caused direct interference in their way of life. Consequently, the Court ordered the annulment of the administrative measure and the realization of the consultation requested by the community.

2.4.4. Colombia Plan: Eradication of Illegal Plantations[159]

The so-called Colombia Plan was conceived during the government of Andrés Pastrana (1998 – 2002) with several political, social, military, and strategic political objectives. It was also approved by the Congress of the United States of America in the context of the 'war on drugs'. An aid proposal for Colombia was presented, which consisted of: (i) pressure on the South, focused on the areas of Putumayo (oil industry) and Caquetá (with strong guerrilla presence) by providing helicopters, artillery, training and assistance in the area of intelligence; (ii) reinforcement of the interdiction in the Andean zone, supporting the installation of radars and air bases, and air force operations through the improvement of airports (including those in Ecuador, Aruba, and Curaçao); (iii) support to the Colombian police force; alternative development to promote the replacement of crops; and (iv) better governance by financing the training of representatives for peace dialogues. The budget of the Colombia Plan was initially set at US$ 1.32 billion, with US$ 860 million for Colombia, of which 74,68% was going directly to military and police support. The estimated total was US$ 7.5 billion, of which US$ 3,52 billion came from abroad, and would be managed by multilateral credit agencies (BM, FMI, BID), and

[159] http://latinoamericana.wiki.br/verbetes/p/plano-colombia, Accessed on 4/06/2017.

the rest would be in charge of the Colombian government. This budget was supplemented with emergency aid at several moments. During the Bush administration – in 2001 – the plan was intensified and became the Andean Counterdrug Initiative, which sought to provide resources for the fight against narcotics in Colombia, Peru, Bolivia, Ecuador, and Brazil.

The Colombia Plan was intended to eradicate coca, poppy, and cannabis plantations in the region by fumigating fields and forests with glyphosate, among other methods of action. The indigenous and traditional communities residing in the areas subjected to fumigation, represented by the Organization of Indigenous Peoples of the Colombian Amazon – OPIAC, proposed legal measures using the argument of violation of their fundamental rights (i) to life, (ii) to communitary existence, (iii) to a healthy environment, (iv) to the free development of personality, (v) to due process, and (vi) to the right of direct participation by indigenous peoples in the decisions that affect them, and that were being violated by the government's illegal crop fumigation programme in their territories. With regard to coca plantations, the indigenous communities of the departments of Putumayo, Guaviare, Guainia, Amazonas, and Caquetá, maintained that such cultivation is traditional, and has been practiced since time immemorial, and that the use of coca in small quantities inside their territories was threatened by indiscriminate fumigation. This case was judged by the Constitutional Court of Colombia, according to sentence SU 383/03.[160]

The first issue the Court faced was the need to demarcate the areas occupied by each one of the indigenous peoples and traditional populations in order to concretely identify the impact and thereby know which peoples should be consulted. As for Prior Consultation, the Court declared that it is a mechanism that, among its goals, serves for the Administration to reflect on the different values in conflict. In this particular case, the Court remarked that the definition itself regarding

[160] http://www.corteconstitucional.gov.co/relatoria/2003/su383-03.htm, Accessed on 04/06/2017.

the role the coca plantations have in the ethnic and cultural life of the community, its essentiality, the survival of the community, as established in the sentence, is a matter that must include the object of Prior Consultation.

The decision argued whether the Consultation can be understood as a veto possibility for indigenous and tribal peoples, and concluded that "it does not imply that indigenous and tribal peoples have the right to veto legal and administrative measures that affect them", being an opportunity for the party states of the Convention to consider and value the positions that members of ethnic minorities have on the proposed actions, forcing a dialogue and, if possible, an agreement. Therefore, consultations cannot be used to impose a decision or to rebut complying with an obligation, but they must be taken as a favourable occasion, not to be wasted, for the government authorities in charge of authorizing, executing, and monitoring the state policy on the eradication of illicit crops, to consider the right of indigenous and tribal peoples to present the respect of the right to cultural integrity and autonomy of their territories as a condition of this policy.

Finally, the Court found that the special protection that is attributed to the right to Prior Consultation consists of carrying out a process whereby the State must guarantee ethnic groups, potentially affected by the undertakings, participation and access to information related to the initiatives or projects, whether of a normative or other character, among which the exploitation of natural resources and/or the construction of civil works that directly affects such communities, or is located in their territories. The mechanism seeks to identify the impact of the projects and with this, protect indigenous and tribal peoples. Therefore, active participation of the communities concerned must be procured in prior discussions, as well as in effective decision-making, which "must be agreed upon, as much as possible".

2.5 Ecuador

As in other South American countries, the discussion over matters related to exploitation industries, especially mining, is very strong, and gave rise to many decisions. Here we will examine two cases considered to be important, that formed important precedents decided by the Constitutional Court of Ecuador.[161]

2.5.1 The Independent Federation of the Shuar People of Ecuador v. the Arco Oriente Company

The Constitutional Court of Ecuador declared a sentence on 16 March 2000, in case 949-99 – RA, a protective appeal filed by the independent federation of the Shuar people of Ecuador versus the Arco Oriente Company.[162] This company owned a concession contract to exploit hydrocarbons in an area of which 70% was situated in indigenous community territory. This concession was granted without any participation of the indigenous community. The company, authorized by contract, entered the indigenous territory and tried to get contracts signed by community members who had no representative power in the group and without respecting the organization modes of the indigenous community. In addition, the plaintiff alleged that the activity performed by the company was based on the use of force, blackmail and other reproachable actions, undermining the unity of the community and its form of organization.

In the first instance, protection was granted and was later confirmed by the Constitutional Court. The following excerpts from the decision are worth mentioning:

> Regarding the indigenous people, it was stated that: "these human groups maintain the occupation and possession over those lands, in which they develop "their traditional forms of conviviality and social organization, of generation and exercise of authority, as expressly determined by item 7 of Article 84 of the Supreme Charter.

And more:

[161] https://www.corteconstitucional.gob.ec/, Accessed on 02/11/2017.

[162] ILO. **La aplicación del convenio núm. 169 por tribunales nacionales e internacionales en América Latina una compilación de casos.** Geneva: ILO, 2009, p. 145-146.

> Discriminatory and unilateral actions by the defendant trigger disagreements between groups in the same community, giving rise to clashes between those who accept the defendant's criteria and those who were either not consulted or disagree with the reasoning of the company, which creates a division in the core of the group. These confrontations, according to the plaintiff, – lead to social fractioning, with internal fission, which may provoke damaging and harmful disculturation in the community.

This was the first legal case filed by an indigenous association that obtained a favourable result from the Ecuadorian courts.

2.5.2 Mining Law

The Constitutional Court, for the transition period, issued another important decision related to the application of Prior Consultation in Sentence no. 001-10-SIN-CC, Cases no. 0008-09-IN and 0011-09-IN (accumulated), 19 March 2010[163] on the occasion of the debates about the constitutionality of the Consultation stipulated in Article 90 of the Mining Law, and in items 7 and 17 of Article 57 of the Constitution, among others, and, if not the case, which are the rules and minimum procedures to be adopted in Prior Consultation to meet the requirements of constitutional provisions? In making explicit the role of the Court during the transition period, the Court stated that:

> The 2008 Constitution establishes a new State form, the Constitutional State of Rights and Justice, whose basic characteristics are: 1) recognition of the superior normative character of the Constitution; 2) the direct application of the Constitution as a legal rule; 3) the recognition of constitutional jurisprudence as a primary source of justice.

Based on the above understanding, the Court initiates an argumentation to deal with the contested rule, from the standpoint of an appropriate interpretation. Regarding the pre-legislative consultation determined in the Constitution, the issue was brought before the court

[163]https://www.corteconstitucional.gob.ec/images/stories/pdfs/SUBE_Y_BAJA/SUBE_Y_BAJA3/Sentencia_mineros.pdf, Accessed on 02/11/2017.

in relation to its formal nature or otherwise. Thus, the Court established that:

> In the Court's opinion, although it is true that pre-legislative consultation is part of the elements that make up the process of approving laws, it is not really a mere procedure or formality. Indeed, according to the Court and in accordance with Article 57 no. 17 of the Constitution of the Republic, pre-legislative consultation constitutes a constitutional right of a collective nature.
>
> (...)
>
> Among the set of collective rights, recognized by the Constitution of Ecuador and pertaining to communes, communities, peoples, and nationalities, are those related to their participation in matters of their concern. However, one of the rights to participation, particularly relevant in this case, is located in Article 57 no. 17 of the Constitution, and establishes that the state is obliged to consult communes, communities, peoples, and nationalities before adopting a legal measure that might affect any of their collective rights, a right that is known among international human rights instruments as 'pre-legislative consultation'.

The Court, in order to make use of the administrative acts practiced by the Administration, moves towards starting to establish the possibility of making exceptions to items 7 and 17 in Article 57, to apply another constitutional article, which must be applied along with Convention 169:

> In fact, based on a textual reading of the aforementioned constitutional precepts, it is clear that the consultations stipulated in items 7 and 17 of Article 57 of the Constitution determine the group to which they must be addressed and, as stated before, as collective rights, their exercise excludes citizens in general.

Based on the above, this Court concludes that the entity who sent the invitation to the President of the Confederation of Indigenous Nationalities of Ecuador, CONAIE, was the Minister of Mines and Oil. Even though the action doesn't comply with Article 57 no. 17 of the Constitution, which stipulates that the organ that must carry out the Prior Consultation is the one with power or powers to adopt legislative measures, that is, the National Assembly, it complies with the text of Article 6 of ILO Convention 169, which states: 'the governments shall: a) consult the peoples concerned, through appropriate procedures and in particular through their representative institutions, whenever consideration is being given to legislative or administrative measures which may affect them directly'.

From this reasoning, the Court goes on to state that since the State carried out the consultation process through the Ministry of Mining and Oil, and in terms of environmental consultations the adopted measure was adequate, it could therefore be used to comply with no. 17 of Article 57:

On the other hand, the aforementioned process, carried out by the Ministry of Mines and Oil, was fully conforming with another one of the processes among those defined in the Constitution, the one stipulated in Article 398 of the Constitution, which is not part of the collective rights of indigenous communities, peoples, and nationalities referred to in Article 57 of the Fundamental Charter. The aforementioned precept clearly establishes that, in the event of possible harm to the environment, the State will be in charge of the consultation.

Therefore, even though the consultation process promoted by the then Minister of Mining and Oil is more consistent with the provision in Article 398 of the Constitution, there is no doubt that, in a certain way, the fact of requesting the participation of a sector of the indigenous communities, peoples, and nationalities, also denotes a direct application of Article 57, no. 17 ,of the Constitution.

After making such clarifications and decisions, the Constitutional Court starts to indicate the parameters that should be taken into consideration for the examination of the contested provision, the Court stated that:

> Even so, there are other sources that allow this Court to establish the minimum necessary parameters that must be met by any participation process so that it can be called 'Prior Consultation' in the terms of no. 7 of Article 57 of the Constitution. Among the most important sources that this Court relies on are the jurisprudence of the Inter-American Court on Human Rights (Saramaca vs. Suriname

> case); the decisions of Courts and Constitutional Courts in the region, such as the Colombian Court (see Constitutional Court Sentence C-161, 2001); the Sentence of the Constitutional Court of Chile (Roll 309 of 4 August 2000); and the recommendations of the ILO specialists committee or the reports of the Special Rapporteur of the United Nations on the rights of indigenous peoples, which are part of what is known as Soft Law and, in this sense, are relevant for Ecuador. Consequently, this Court will make use of the general recommendations of Special Rapporteur James Anaya regarding the minimal requirements the consultation process must meet to deserve this name.

According to the Ecuadorian Court, the specific parameters that must be taken into consideration are those included in Convention 169, namely:

1. The flexible character of the consultation procedure, according to the national law of each country and to the tradition, uses, and customs of the consulted peoples.
2. The prior nature of the Consultation, that is, every process must have a beginning and an end before any stage of the mining activity.
3. The public and informed character of the Consultation, that is, the participants must have opportune and complete access to the information necessary to understand the effects of the mining activities on their lands.
4. The recognition that the Consultation does not end with mere information or the public dissemination of information.
5. The Consultation must be a systematic negotiation process that guarantees a genuine dialogue with the legitimate representatives of each party.
6. All involved parties have the obligation to act in good faith throughout the process, seeking consensus between the involved parties.
7. That the dissemination and a reasonable timeframe are ensured for each of the stages of the Prior Consultation process.
8. Prior and consensual definition of the procedure to be adopted.

9. Prior definition of the subjects (people and communities) to be consulted.
10. Respect for the social and representative structures of the consulted parties.
11. The systematic and formal character of the Consultation, including documentation etc.

In conclusion, the Court decides:

> 1 - To declare that, in the absence of a ruling body that regulates the parameters of a pre-legislative consultation, the information and participation process implemented before the issuing of the Mining Law was developed as a direct application of the Constitution; consequently, the argument of formal unconstitutionality of the Mining Law is rejected.
>
> 2. That pre-legislative consultation is of a substantial and non-formal nature.

2. 6 Peru

Like other South American constitutional courts, the Peruvian Constitutional Court has ruled on several issues based on Convention 169.[164] It is important to remark that Peru already recognized indigenous communities from its 1920 Constitution onward (Articles 41 and 58), and is one of the pioneers on the matter. What follows are some relevant cases, chosen in view of the main goal of this work, which is the examination of Prior Consultation with indigenous and tribal peoples.

2.6.1 The Inter-ethnic Association for the Development of the Peruvian Forest (AIDESEP)

With Sentence STC 06316-2008-PA/TCO of 11 November 2009,[165] the Peruvian Constitutional Court ruled on the Constitutional Review Appeal filed by the Inter-ethnic Association for the Development of the

[164]http://www.tc.gob.pe/jurisprudencia/2011/00024-2009-AI.html, Accessed on 08/06/2017.
[165]https://tc.gob.pe/jurisprudencia/2010/06316-2008-AA.pdf, Accessed on 04/11/2017.

Peruvian Forest (AIDESEP) against Resolution no. 53 of the Mixed Civil Chamber of the Superior Court of Justice of Loreto, which judged the protective action filed against the Ministry of Mining and Energy and the companies Perupetro S.A., Barret Resource Perú Corporation, and Repsol YPF to be unfounded.

The issue was related to a permit grant for the exploitation of two plots located in indigenous lands, by means of Decrees 028/1999 of 7 July 1999 and 038/195 of 10 December 1995, which, as understood by the plaintiff's association, violated indigenous rights to life, health, well-being, ethnic integrity, a balanced environment, property, ancestral ownership, natural resources, as well as the right to the intangibility of the territory – the future reserve of indigenous peoples in a situation of voluntary isolation - Waorani (Tagaeri-Taromenane), Pananujuri (Arabela), and Aushiris or Abijiras, all them occupants of the area covered by the Napo Tigre Territorial Reserve Proposal. Finally, the plaintiff argued that the indigenous peoples were not priorly consulted about the issuing of the decrees, which then required the suspension of all activities of oil production and exploration, as well as ceasing to contact indigenous peoples in voluntary isolation.

The defense maintained that the decrees ensured the exercise of economic freedom guaranteed by the Constitution, that the plaintiff's association did not present any evidence that the activities of oil production and exploration had effectively harmed the indigenous communities and, especially, those uncontacted communities; that an environmental impact study had been approved by the administrative authority in charge; that there had been proper consultation with indigenous peoples, who had not confirmed that the contested activities were in fact harmful to the autochtone communities or the environment; that halting the activities would result in income loss for for the State; that it is up to the State to decide on the concession of natural resources for economic exploitation and not to the Judiciary; that licensing contracts are subject to Article 62 of the Peruvian Constitution and cannot be altered; that, finally, indigenous peoples in voluntary isolation had been acknowledged and that the Napo Tigre

Territorial Reserve Proposal doesn't have legal power since it does not exist in the legal world.

The Court, in examining the specific issue of the Consultation, affirmed that:

> 65 - Although if it is not for this Court to evaluate the quality of said informative meetings, it is clear that the requirement imposed by ILO Convention 169 is for a prior, public, neutral, and transparent consultation, whose convocation must be made in the same language as the corresponding communities and with the supervision of state entities that ensure the quality of the provided information and with reasonable levels of participation of the members of the community and their representatives, a consultation in which community members are not reduced to be mere receivers of information, rather, it must encourage their participation by taking into consideration their points of view on the consulted matters. These minimum conditions required by the right to consultation were not presented in the present case, which in principle would lead to declaring this extreme of the appeal to be well founded. Nevertheless, the case forced us to reflect upon the eventual consequences that such a decision would have in the face of the constitutional goods at stake.

Therefore, as we can see, after pointing out the elements that must be present for the Consultation to be legally and constitutionally valid, the Court proceeded with the specific case and compared the right to Consultation with other rights of a constitutional nature, affirming that:

> 68 – Aside from all this, considering the operations of these companies were taken within the framework of Contract Law, signed with the Peruvian State and guaranteed by Article no. 62 of the Constitution. Therefore, in announcing the decision on this case, this Collegiate must consider the effects of their decision so as not to generate further sacrifices than those they intend to caution against.
>
> 70 – Reflecting on the effects of the sentence is part of the duties of this Court. The basis of such competence is found both in the character of guarantor of the rights it holds, that is, of all rights the Constitution recognizes, which must be carried out according to the

> principle of practical concordance, but also in its autonomy as a judicial body of the State. In this regard, it was established that "compliance with the principle of autonomy, recognized in Article 201 of the Constitution, [this Court] has the power to procedurally modulate the content and effects of its sentences in all constitutional processes in general, and in protective actions in particular". (STC no. 05033 - 2006 - AA-TC, foundation 62).
>
> 71 - This is why this Collegiate considers that the right to Consultation must, in this case, be put in operation gradually by the companies involved and under the supervision of the competent entities. With this, the Court will determine that a plan of shared commitments between the private companies is to be set in motion, they will not see their works paralyzed, and the communities themselves and their leaders also cannot renounce their rights and they must be reinstated as quickly as possible, thus opening up a dialogue to build a space of harmony and mutual trust.

As we can see, even though the Constitutional Court confirmed the right to Consultation, in this specific case it chose to modulate the effects of the decision in order to equally safeguard other rights, on a constitutional level, and evidently, the contracts signed between the Peruvian government and third parties. The Court considered the existence of two constitutionally protected rights, being certain that one doesn't prevail over the other and that there must be harmony between them both. It must be remarked that in this specific case, no severe harm to indigenous peoples was proven, which is why the decision of the Constitutional Court seems to be in letter and spirit of Convention 169.

2.6.2 Legislative Decree 994

In 2011, citizen Gonzalo Tuanama Tuanama and another 6226 citizens obtained a final decision over a legal claim of unconstitutionality (EXP. N.º 00024-2009-PI), which contested Legislative Decree 994, whose objective was related to the promotion of private investments in irrigation projects and expansion of the Peruvian farming border, published on 13 March 2008. According to the arguments presented by the plaintiffs, the measure was unconstitutional because:

(i) The Legislative Decree was issued without Prior, Free and Informed Consultation with indigenous peoples, as established by ILO Convention 169 and Articles 19, 30, and 32 of the United Nations Declaration on the Rights of Indigenous Peoples, so,

(ii) There was a violation of Article 118, I of the Peruvian Constitution. According to the plaintiff's arguments, Legislative Decree no. 994 incentivizes irrigation projects on uncultivated lands, with the exception of those with communal or private property titles; therefore, communities with no titles, even if with a history of ancestral possession, could be displaced by the implementation of said projects. The plaintiffs added that the simple immemorial possession of their territories is sufficient to grant them property, which must be recognized by the State, as it has already been widely recognized by the Inter-American Court on Human Rights in cases concerning indigenous peoples.

In response, the Peruvian government sustained, among other things, that ILO Convention 169 is not applicable in Peru, given that the country has a predominantly mestizo population and that a large part of the rural population has ancestral indigenous origins, however, with the development of civilization, becoming mixed, and it is arbitrary to frame all rural and native populations as indigenous peoples. As a result, it is necessary to adapt Convention 169 to the Peruvian reality. Ergo, the Legislative Decree is not unconstitutional because it didn't determine the accomplishment of Prior Consultation.

The Court found that its jurisprudence, in cases motivated by social conflict after the year 2009, has sought to affirm the *constitutional value* of the right to Prior Consultation of indigenous peoples, which serves to guarantee a set of specific fundamental constitutional rights derived from a constitutional level-treaty, C 169, as established by court precedents (STC 6316-2008-PA/TC and STC 5427-2009-PC/TC). The Court understands that the right to Consultation is constituted by a series of 'fundamental' positions, which, according to decision STC 0022-2009-PI/TC, Fund. Jur. no. 37, are the following:

(i) the collective right to be consulted in the face of state measures that directly affect their collective interests or rights, particularly those regarding their physical existence, cultural identity, quality of life, or their collective development;

(ii) the right for Consultation to be carried out in advance and according to the principles of good faith, flexibility, transparency, respect, and interculturality, and

(iii) the right that the agreements derived from the Consultation process are complied with, "excluding from this legal programme the right to consultation which became popularly known as 'the right to veto'."

Based on the above arguments, the Constitutional Court found that the right to Consultation is not an individual right – it is worth remembering here that despite the large number of plaintiffs, the claim had an individual nature – but is rather of a collective nature, and should be properly requested by the representative entities of the indigenous peoples, "being constitutionally mandatory whenever the State foresees legal or administrative measures that might affect them directly". The Court added that in abstract terms it cannot be determined when a measure directly affects indigenous peoples, in any case, it is not hard to notice that it includes any state measures – administrative or legislative – whose effect is to "diminish, jeopardize, unfavourably influence or provoke a direct alteration in the collective rights and interests of indigenous peoples'.

The Constitutional Court, in order to identify the mentioned measures, established three standards:

(i) measures aimed at regulating situations that exclusively concern indigenous peoples;

(ii) rules of a general scope that may imply an 'indirect' impact on indigenous peoples; and

(iii) specific measures related to indigenous peoples within the rules of general application [STC 0022-2009-PI/TC, Fund. Jur. No. 21].

Contradicting the government's allegations, the Constitutional Court finds that the enforceability of the right to Consultation is defined in Convention 169 and must be observed.

2.6.3 Unconstitutionality appeal filed by Gonzalo Tuanama Tuanama, representing more than five thousand citizens against Legislative Decree no. 1089[166] (Exp. no. 0022-2009-PI/TC).

Gonzalo Tuanama Tuanama, representing more than five thousand citizens, filed a claim against Legislative Decree no. 1089 which regulates the Extraordinary Temporal Regime for the Formalization and Titling of Rural Buildings. According to the plaintiffs' allegations, the aforementioned decree was issued without the necessary Prior and Informed Consultation with indigenous peoples, as determined by ILO Convention 169, thus violating fundamental rights of indigenous peoples such as (i) the right to Prior Consultation and (ii) the collective right to ancestral territory guaranteed by Articles 6, 15, 17, and 19 of Convention 169, andand Articles 19, 30, and 32 of the United Nations Declaration on the Rights of Indigenous Peoples were violated as well. They also argued that Article 118, 1 of the Peruvian Constitution and Articles 70 and 88 of the Political Charter were disrespected.

In response to the contestation, the Executive Power argued that:

(i) the contested Decree created a mechanism to simplify the procedures for the formalization of rural property, thus enabling farmers to obtain ownership over the lands they occupy and that, through the real estate registry, greater legal security to their properties was guaranteed;

(ii) the Decree did not exceed the limits of Law no. 29.157;

[166] http://heinerantonioriverarodriguez.blogspot.com.br/2011/04/expediente-0022-2009-pi-tc-gonzalo.html, Accessed on 05/11/2017.

(iii) the Decree did not derogate from Law no. 22.175 on native communities and the Agrarian Development of Forest and Forest Margins, for the Decree is transitory and it did not make mention of the fundamental rights of indigenous peoples;

(iv) the United Nations Declaration on the Rights of Indigenous Peoples was not signed by Peru, therefore it is not part of the national legal framework, and has no binding effects for the Peruvian state;

(v) the application of ILO Convention 169 should not be mentioned, for the Peruvian population is predominantly mestiza and the peasant populations which were originally indigenous, with the development of civilization are now mestizas, as is the case with the peasant populations on the coast and in the Andean valleys of the mountains.

(vi) Therefore, it would be arbitrary to attribute indigenous status to such communities;

(vii) there is no unconstitutionality of Decree 1089 – nor any other legal norm – for the simple fact that Prior Consultation with indigenous peoples was not carried out, given that there is no law that establishes who are Peruvian indigenous peoples, which matters must be submitted to Prior Consultation, and what procedure should be adopted in those cases, and finally

(viii) that the Decree is directed towards general application, it is not directly binding to one single community.

As a basis for its decision, the Constitutional Court recalled that Article 2, section 2 of the Peruvian Constitution indicates that the recognition and tolerance of diversity are values intrinsic to the Constitutional Text.

> In this sense, individuals cannot be arbitrarily differentiated and harmed by reasons based on, among others, their opinion, religion, or language. Therefore, any forced homogenization that disrespects or threatens singularities of people identifiable by any constitutionally relevant criterion must be eradicated. As such, we seek to build a unity based on diversity, considering the right to

> equality as a protector of different manifestations of the human personality.
>
> In this sense, individuals cannot be arbitrarily differentiated. This is why the Constitution, erected on the recognition of a person's dignity, from which the principles of freedom, equality, and solidarity emanate, must be conceived from a pluralist conception that protects the different ways of perceiving and acting in reality. Therefore, in STC 0042- AI/TC, this Court affirmed that "the 1993 Constitution recognized the human person as a member of a multicultural and multi-ethnic state". Thus, the existence of indigenous peoples and ancestral and originary cultures of Peru is not unknown' [Fund. 1]. But not only isn't it unknown, but the Constitution obliges their tutelage and protection. This way, the particularity and complexity of the protection of minority ethnic groups led to the adoption of specific constitutional measures for their defense.

As decided by the Court, the claim that Peru is a mestizo nation was refused on the basis of consolidated precedents and, evidently, on the Constitutional Text itself which is quite clear regarding the multi-ethnic character of Peruvian society. Regarding the arguments put forward by the Peruvian state that both the United Nations Declaration on the Rights of Indigenous Peoples and Convention 169 of the International Labour Organization were inapplicable to the specific case, the Constitutional Court also rejected them, with the following legal construction:

> 7. Regarding the UNDRIP, it must be taken into account that the General Assembly of the United Nations Organization approved the 'Declaration on the Rights of Indigenous People' on 13 September 2007, of which the text was approved with 143 votes in favour, 4 in contrary, and 11 abstentions. This document contains 46 articles which establish legal principles on the rights of indigenous peoples. It is a document of international law, and it must also be considered that it is a declaration and not a treaty, therefore ratification does not apply. Nevertheless, it must be added that declarations represent a widespread agreement and consensus in the international community. Indeed, as an outcome of negotiations and acceptance

> by the majority of the General Assembly of the United Nations, it possesses a moral weight and also offers an evident orientation of the international community towards the respect and protection of indigenous peoples, by establishing the content of human rights in the context of indigenous peoples.
>
> 8. The content of the declaration is not mandatorily binding, which does not imply that it has no legal consequence. Declarations represent goals and objectives to which the international community strives. In international law it is known as Soft Law, that is, a guide that still has legal repercussions even though it isn't binding to the State. Its content represents a code of conduct without being legally binding. In this sense, the UNDRIP will be considered by this Court as a rule with a Soft Law character, without generating a conventional obligation on the part of the Peruvian State.

Regarding the applicability of Convention 169, the Constitutional Court finds that Convention 169 is part of the Peruvian legal framework and, like any other rule, must be obeyed. On the other hand, "international treaties on human rights not only conform to our framework, but, moreover, they boast a constitutional level" (STC No. 0025-2005-PI/TC, Fundament 33).

In the Constitutional Court's understanding, Convention 169 doesn't require regulating, for it is of immediate applicability:

> 11.....The underlying issue of this argument is that the aforementioned Convention would be a programmatic provision and cannot be applied without first having domestic regulations that develop it. In this respect, such an approach can be questioned from two different perspectives. First, assuming the Executive Power's claim that it is a programmatic provision, we must bear in mind that the Convention was signed by the Peruvian State in 1994, coming into force in 1995. In other words, fifteen years passed until it was enforced today,was enforced today, due to the exclusive responsibility of the State. This argument only exposes an omission by the State and therefore must be rejected. In any case, this Court doesn't ignore that on 19 May 2010, Congress approved the Law on the Right to Prior Consultation of Indigenous or Native Peoples

> recognized by ILO Convention 169, which is an important step forward in protecting the right to consultation.
>
> 12. Secondly, it is not a constitutionally valid argument to deny the application of fundamental rights due to the absence of legal or infralegal regulation. This would leave the application of fundamental rights in the hands of the discretionary power of the State, a position which conflicts with the Constitutional State of Law, in which the Constitution engages the whole of society, including the constitutional bodies or so-called Powers of State. From this perspective, its programmatic or self-applicable nature doesn't have further impact, since the fact is that, due to a provisionary omission, the exercise of a series of fundamental rights of a part of society is denied. Furthermore, in the case of international commitments, Articles 26 and 27 of the Vienna Convention on the Law of Treaties must be taken into consideration. The first article states that: "Every treaty in force is binding upon the parties to it and must be performed by them in good faith." The second article indicates that; "A party may not invoke the provisions of its internal law as justification for its failure to perform a treaty." Although in this case the violation of Convention 169 is not justified on the basis of an internal law provision, it intends to justify it based on an omission, a situation that can be interpreted as subsumed in the terms of the mandate of Article 27 of the aforementioned Convention.

The Court developed a very interesting argument when dealing with the issue of Prior Consultation regarding administrative and legal measures that could affect indigenous peoples, stating that:

> 19. Article 6 of the Convention demands that indigenous peoples be consulted when, in applying its provisions, legal or administrative measures that may affect them directly are envisaged. Moreover, despite the fact that in the case of administrative resolutions, the task of identifying the administrative measure that can directly affect indigenous peoples is not so complex – due to the particular aspect that administrative measures usually have –, in relation to legal measures, the task is extremely complicated. It can be quite simple to determine that a rule, like the Law of Private Investment in the Development of Economic Activities in the Lands of National

Territory and of Native and Peasant Communities (Law no. 26505), will probably affect indigenous peoples directly, since it implies relevant changes to their legal status. There are, however, other types of laws whose analysis is not so simple.

20. In effect, a law of a general scope, aimed at regulating the conduct of all Peruvian citizens, and not particularly the conduct of indigenous peoples, would not imply a direct impact on indigenous peoples. Even though it could lead to a change in the legal status of indigenous peoples, that would be a consequence or an indirect effect of the rule. For example, issuing a civil code or a criminal procedure code, although it may affect indigenous peoples, must in principle be considered as a rule that would only have an indirect impact, and is therefore exempt from going through the process of consultation with indigenous peoples.

21 – In this context, three types of legislative measures can be observed, which exclusively aim to regulate relevant aspects of indigenous peoples, and when consultation will be mandatory, since they all affect them directly. On the other hand, there are laws of a general nature which could have an indirect impact on indigenous peoples. The third type of legal measure is one in which certain issues involving legislation of general nature require establishing, in some points, specific references to indigenous peoples. In these cases, if these normative alterations directly modify the legal status of indigenous peoples, in relevant matters and in a substantial way, of course these points must be subject to Consultation.

This way, Consultation related to legislative measures is only effective in the event that it is a bill specifically aimed at regulating aspects of indigenous peoples lives, or, in the case of a law of a general character, that its concrete effects may have a direct impact on the lives of indigenous peoples.

Another relevant point the decision confronts is related to the assumed veto right of indigenous peoples over activities that might affect their territories. In that respect, the Court found that:

24. From the reading of Articles 6 and 15 of Convention 169 it is not apparent that indigenous peoples have a kind of right of veto. That is, the State's obligation of consulting indigenous peoples

> regarding legislative or administrative measures that may directly affect them doesn't grant them the capacity to prevent such measures from coming into effect. Even though the last paragraph of Article 6 of the Convention says the Consultation must be carried out "with the purpose of reaching an agreement or obtaining consent on the proposed measures", that doesn't mean it is a condition, that when not reached, means the measure is rejected. What this article explains is the goal must be to guide, this must be the purpose of the Consultation. This implies that a Consultation process that doesn't intend to reach such a goal can be questioned. It must be stated that the articles of the Convention don't express that indigenous peoples have a right to veto. The intention of the rule is institutionalizing intercultural dialogue.

As for the constitutionality of the Decree, the Constitutional Court stated that:

> 56. In accordance with the principle of preserving the law - which requires the constitutional judge to 'save', to the extent possible, the constitutionality of a disputed law [STC 004-2004-CC / TC, fundo, 3.3] - the interpretation of the legal norm must be reflected upon. Because the declaration of unconstitutionality only applies in the case of evident unconstitutionality and whenever there is no other decision or interpretation possible. Therefore, in observing that this legal norm allows us to interpret that the scope of its articles excludes indigenous peoples, this is how the legal norm must be understood or interpreted. In this way, and only this way, the legal norm is constitutional, since this regulation is not aimed at indigenous peoples. In conclusion, the legal norm under analysis here is constitutional insofar as indigenous peoples are excluded from its reach, otherwise the legal norm would have to be submitted to the Consultation process.

2.7 Venezuela

Venezuela, in Article 120 of its current Constitution, combined with Articles 53/61 of the Organic Law on Indigenous Peoples and Communities, establishes the right to Prior Consultation with indigenous peoples in the event of exploitation of natural resources in their territories. However, while researching the topic with the Venezuelan Superior Court of Justice, it was not possible to find decisions on the matter. Essentially, the discussion on Prior, Free, and Informed Consultation in Venezuela is sparse.

In fact, there has been no Consultation procedure with indigenous peoples in Venezuela since 1999.[167]

3 Prior consultation before Brazilian Judicial Power

3.1 General Observations

Brazil is a signatory of Convention 169, which was incorporated into Brazilian domestic law by Decree no. 5.051, of 19 April 2004. In the thirteen or so years since the adoption of the Convention, as in other countries of South America, the volume of legal disputes related to the application of the Convention has been increasing, especially in matters of Prior Consultation. The main protagonist in such disputes is the Federal Public Ministry, which maintains a strategic alliance with indigenous peoples and traditional populations that stems from an express constitutional determination, contained in Article 129,V. The Federal Justice Portal[168] presents 79 entries for "ILO 169", which indicates that the Convention has been strongly debated in Brazilian federal courts. This subchapter doesn't intend to carry out an exhaustive study of all judicial decisions related to the application of Convention 169, which would be a vain claim. Thus, we opted for the actions that reached the higher courts (STF and STJ [*Supremo Tribunal Federal* - Federal Supreme Court, and *Superior Tribunal de Justiça* - Superior Court of Justice]), especially the STF. We will briefly present the cases of AHE Belo Monte (state of Pará) and the Quingoma quilombola community (state of Bahia). Nevertheless, given the chronic slowness of the Brazilian judicial system, the manifestations of the superior Courts in the

[167] Grupo de Trabajo Asuntos Indígenas de la ULA, Provea, Laboratorio de Paz: Lexys Rendón Situación del **Derecho a la Consulta Previa** en Venezuela (2016), Caracas, p. 42.
[168] http://www.cjf.jus.br/juris/unificada, Accessed on 04/10/2017. Only presents selected decisions of the RFCs.

majority of cases constitute decisions aimed at procedural issues, delivered in isolation by their presidents, with the purpose of revoking preliminary measures and anticipated protective measures issued by lower courts.

The importance of indigenous lands to indigenous peoples and traditional populations has been widely discussed throughout this text, and it is particularly necessary to present the current prevailing conception of the Federal Supreme Court on the matter, which we will do with a brief exposition on the Raposa Serra do Sol Indigenous Land case, situated in the state of Roraima.

3. 2 Federal Supreme Court

Just as the other Constitutional Courts in South America, the Brazilian Federal Supreme Court has faced issues related to Consultation as established by Convention 169, as well as matters related to indigenous peoples in general. In particular, it is important to remark that Brazilian Constitutional Law has recognized the existence of specific rights of indigenous peoples since 1934, which has generated a significant number of judicial decisions related to the indigenous matter. On this topic, as we did with other South-American countries, we will choose some decisions that we consider more appropriate to expose our subject matter. Because of its importance to the indigenous topic in general, the decision on the important case of Raposa Serra do Sol Indigenous Land will be addressed.

3.2.1 Raposa Serra do Sol Indigenous Land

Raposa Serra do Sol Indigenous Land[169] is located in Roraima state, which was created by the Federal Constitution of 1988 when the former federal territory of Roraima was transformed into a state. The Indigenous Land covers an area of 1.743.089 hectares, and is inhabited

[169] https://terrasindigenas.org.br/en/terras-indigenas/3835, Accessed on 08/10/2017.

by five indigenous peoples who make up a total population of 23.119 people.

People	Linguistic Family	Language
Ingarikó	Karib	Ingarikó
Macuxi	Karib	Macuxi
Patamona	Karib	Patamona
Taurepang	Karib	Taulipáng(Pemóng))
Wapichana	Aruak	Wapichana

The importance of Raposa Serra do Sol Indigenous Land in Roraima state can be shown by the amount of municipalities situated in its interior, as the chart below demonstrates:

Municipalities - Raposa Serra do Sol Indigenous Land

#	FU [federal unit]	Municipality	Municipal Area (ha)	% of the municipality covered by the Indigenous Land
1	RR	Normandia	696,678.00	97.12 %
2	RR	Pacaraima	802,843.00	32.49 %
3	RR	Uiramutã	806,552.00	100,00 %

The legal decision of the Federal Superior Court appeared in the records of a popular lawsuit which had been underway for years within the Federal Justice and which questioned the Indigenous Land by arguing that its confirmation and definition would put "Roraima's development at risk". Thus, the Federal Supreme Court started to discuss the criteria that legitimized the demarcation of the Indigenous Land, making use of the so-called 'time frame' for the establishment of the *dies a quo* for the beginning of the traditional indigenous occupation. On that occasion, the Federal Supreme Court defined as *dies a quo* the date of the promulgation of the Federal Constitution of 1988 (5 October 1988) which, for that reason, came to be the date of the initial time count of the land occupation by the indigenous peoples and the definition of the traditionality of its occupation, as expressed in the following excerpt of the vote declared by Minister Carlos Ayres de Brito (STF, Pet. 3388):

> "**I. - the time frame of the occupation**. Here, we must see that our Major Law worked with a certain date: the date of its own promulgation (5 October 1988) as an irreplaceable reference for the recognition, to the indians, of "the rights over the lands they traditionally occupy"" Lands they traditionally **occupy**, pay attention, and not those they come to occupy. Nor the lands already occupied in other times, but without enough continuity to reach the objective framework of 5 October 1988. The objective framework reflects the decided constitutional purpose of once and for all putting a stop to the endless discussions about any other temporal reference for the occupation of indigenous areas. Even though such reference was written in the previous Constitution. It is expressed: **the date of the verification of the fact of the land occupation itself is 5 October 1988, and no other**. With this we avoid, at the same time: a) the fraud of the subtânea proliferation of indigenous villages, including by recruiting indians from other parts of Brazil, sometimes even from other countries, with the sole purpose of artificializing the expansion of demarcation boundaries [our highlight]; b) the violence of expelling indians in order to mischaracterize the traditionality of their land ownership, to the date of the current Constitution. In a word, the moment when the new Brazilian Fundamental Law comes into force, is the **x-ray image** of the indigenous matter of this delicate topic of land occupation to be demarcated by the Union, for the permanent possession and usufruct of this or that aboriginal ethnicity. Exclusive **use and fruition** (that is what usufruct is, according to Pontes de Miranda) regarding the "riches of the soil, rivers, and lakes" within the area that is the object of precise demarcation (Paragraph 2, Article 231), because the "mineral resources, including those of the subsoil" are already part of another

> category of "Union goods" (section IX of Article 20 of the FC); II – **the time frame of the traditionality of the occupation .** It is not enough, however, to acknowledge a land occupation which coincides with the day and year of the promulgation of our Carta Magna. It is still necessary that it is collectively situated in a certain area with a lasting character. But this is a **traditionally** qualified type of durability of the indigenous occupation, in a spiritual and psychological sense, in that living in a certain area is as much about them belonging to the land as it is the land belonging to the indians ('Anna Pata, Anna Yan': 'Nossa Terra, Nossa Mãe')."

Although it is pragmatic, the decision deserves criticism. In effect, the Constitution defined indigenous rights as 'originary' and declared null all actions that in some way intended to alienate, change, transfer them, and so on. It is known that in many cases there is indeed a 'fabrication' of indigenous villages and areas by ill-intended indigenous people. However, these occurrences are not in any way comparable to the violent expulsion of indigenous peoples from their lands, which often happens. Moreover, a quick glance at Brazilian history shows that this latter circumstance is far more frequent than the former. In fact, constitutional recognition of the rights of indigenous peoples over the lands they occupy dates from the 1934 Constitution. Therefore, it seems reasonable to set the *dies a quo* for the recognition of indigenous possession on the day of the promulgation of the 1934 Constitution of (16 July 1934). There are historical documents that can easily demonstrate if a certain population was expelled from their lands after 1934 and, thus, depending on the specific case, their return is a matter of justice. The establishment of the so-called time frame of 5 October 1988 can serve to legitimize a lot of past violence and illegal occupation, even if this was not the Supreme Federal Court's desire. Finally, it is worth remembering Rojas, Yamada, and Oliveira's criticism[170] of the decision, which, in their opinion:

[170] ROJAS, Biviany Garzón; YAMADA, Erika M and OLIVEIRA, Rodrigo. **Direito à consulta e consentimento de povos indígenas, quilombolas e comunidades tradicionais**. São Paulo: Rede de Cooperação Amazônica – RCA ; Washington, DC : Due Process of Law Foundation, 2016, p. 10.

'[the decision] also relativized the indians' rights to the exclusive usufruct of natural resources available in their territories. It established a set of 'safeguards' or 'conditions' of the decision that is not compatible with the constitutional right to the exclusive usufruct by the indigenous peoples over their territories...'

Nonetheless, we cannot deny the importance of the decision and the fact that it has effectively established operational parameters for the legal administration of the issue of indigenous lands.

3.2.2 Belo Monte

Due to the great geographic expansion of its jurisdiction area, which encompasses the states of Acre, Amapá, Amazonas, Bahia, Federal District, Goiás, Maranhão, Mato Grosso, Minas Gerais, Pará, Piauí, Rondônia, Roraima, and Tocantins, the Federal Regional Court of the First Region is certainly the Brazilian Court that has ruled on the largest number of claims from indigenous peoples and traditional populations related to the application of Convention 169, registering monocratic decisions and judgments that add up to a total of 55 legal decisions. The main issues have also been raised before the judicial sections that make up the jurisdiction area of the Federal Regional Court of the First Region, because the entire Amazonian region is under its jurisdiction.

One of the pioneering decisions of the Federal Regional Court of the First Region is about the construction of the hydroelectric power plant Belo Monte. Concerning the debate over Article 231, Paragraph 3 of the Federal Constitution, on that occasion the RFC[171] found that:

"it sets out two prerequisites for the exploitation of hydric resources, including those with energetic potential, which are: authorization from the National Congress and the hearing of affected communities. It doesn't state, however, the precedence of one measure over the other".

[171] 0000709-88.2006.4.01.3903. AC 2006.39.03.000711-8 / PA. Relatora Desembargadora Federal Selene Maria de Almeida Relator para Acórdão Desembargador Federal Fagundes de Deus, 5ª Turma, Publication: 25/11/2011 e-DJF1 P. 566. Date: 09/11/2011.

Based on this statement, the Court moves towards the conclusion that:

> 'considering the principle of reasonability, it must be concluded that the hearing of communities located in the area of influence of the enterprise can only take place after the completion of the respective studies (EIA/RIMA), even because it is in these studies that the enterprise's strategies will be defined, to mitigate environmental impact and define the actual repercussions of the project.'

Here we see an evident contradiction with the provisions of Convention 169, which in its Article 6 (1) (a) defines Consultation to be prior. In effect, the Consultation with indigenous peoples must be prior to the projects' implementation and must also consider the planning stage, as it is the responsibility of governments to "consult the peoples concerned, through appropriate procedures and in particular through their representative institutions, whenever consideration is being given to legislative or administrative measures which may affect them directly". Therefore, the affirmation that "the hearing of communities located in the area of influence of the enterprise can only take place after the completion of the respective studies" is outside of the context of Convention 169. In fact, the process is continuous and is not defined by an isolated and formal act that can be temporarily identified as a unique activity.

With regard to the congressional act that authorized the implementation of the Belo Monte hydroelectric power plant in indigenous territory, the decision added that:

> "The congressional act under discussion also is not offensive to Convention 169 of the International Labour Organization (ILO) on Indigenous and Tribal Peoples, whose norms establish consultation with indians over legal and administrative measures that may directly affect them. This is because, in this specific case, the hearing of affected communities actually took place, as amply clarified in the memorandum presented by FUNAI itself and demonstrated by documents in the records of the proceedings, since, at several moments, consultations were held with local communities, not only indigenous but also with riverbank dwellers. *On the other hand, the*

legal norms written in such a convention do not establish that the Consultation with indigenous peoples must be prior to authorization by the National Congress. It even highlights the effectiveness of these meetings with the aforementioned communities, so much so that the project, referred to as the enterprise, underwent different alterations, resulting from mitigating and controlling the damage of actions that could result from implementing the hydroelectric power plant in the region."

Legislative Decree 788/2005, authorizing the implementation of the Belo Monte hydroelectric power plant in indigenous territory, was 'confirmed' by the Federal Regional Court of the First Region and later by the Federal Supreme Court; however, as can be verified in its terms, a legislative decree is limited to reproducing environmental licensing requirements and, in fact, was not preceded with the necessary 'appropriate' and 'good will' debate with indigenous peoples and traditional populations as determined by Convention 169. Besides, in this particular case, it is worth recalling the decision delivered by the Colombian Constitutional Court (Sentence C-175/09), which ruled that the Rural Development Statute (Law 1.152/07) was unconstitutional for violating Articles 2, 7, 40, and 330 of the Colombian Constitution and Article 6 of Convention 169, due to lack of Consultation with indigenous and Afro-descendent communities when drafting the bill or during its processing within Congress. Nevertheless, in analyzing other decisions of South American Constitutional Courts, we observe that the main tendency is to modulate the effects of the decision, taking advantage of the legislative act and making necessary corrections.

The discussion about the Belo Monte hydroelectric power plant involves 25 different lawsuits[172] at different stages of development. However, it is necessary to note that the power plant is already operating commercially, even though not at full capacity.[173] The Federal Supreme

[172]http://www.mpf.mp.br/pa/sala-de-imprensa/documentos/2016/tabela_de_acompanhamento_belo_monte_atualizada_mar_2016.pdf/, Accessed on 07/10/2017.
[173]http://g1.globo.com/economia/noticia/2016/04/belo-monte-inicia-operacao-comercial-6-anos-apos-ser-licitada.html, Accessed on 07/10/2017.

Court, through the Suspension of Injunction 125/PA, announced by the Chief Justice of the SFC (16/02/2007), in essence, confirmed the decision of RFC 1, given it had been suspended by an Interlocutory Appeal which, in granting suspension to the Federal Public Ministry's appeal, also suspended the effects of the Interlocutory Appeal which, in turn, revoked the previously granted injunction in the records of Public Civil Action 2006.39.03.000711-8, filed by the Federal Public Ministry before the Federal Court of Altamira/PA. Subsequently, IBAMA filed a Precautionary Measure in a Complaint[174] before the Federal Supreme Court, claiming that the Federal Public Ministry had filed the Public Civil Action with the intention of paralyzing the administrative activities related to the conduct of the licencing process of the Belo Monte power plant, under the grounds of nullity of Legislative Decree no. 788/2005, due to the existence of formal flaws. In this specific case, the Federal Supreme Court maintained the validity of the contested Legislative Decree, by means of a decision and in agreement with what was decided in SL 125.

3.2.3 Quingoma Quilombola Community

Another interesting case is the Suspension of Anticipated Tutelage STA 856 / BA - BAHIA[175] which was 'not acknowledged' by the Court on the grounds that any offenses to Convention 169 do not constitute a direct violation of constitutional norms, especially those considered in Articles 216, 225, and 231 of the Federal Constitution and Article 68 of the ADCT. The issue under debate referred to the environmental licensing of a highway in Bahia state (BA - 099), in which there was a discussion on the land tenure regularization of a remaining community from the Quingoma quilombo. The Public Civil Action intended to stop the environmental licensing procedure until the regularization of

[174] STF. 14404 MC / DF - Author: Min. AYRES BRITTO. Trial: 27/08/2012.DJe-171 Declaration: 29/08/2012. Publication: 30/08/2012.

[175] STF Suspensão de Tutela Antecipada 856/BA. Author: Min. Presidente Trial: 01/03/2017 Decision Declared by Min. CÁRMEN LÚCIA. DJe-043. Declaration: 07/03/2017. Publication: 08/03/2017.

the quilombola territory was done. Ithad already been recognized by the Palmares Foundation. One of the main arguments of the measure's plaintiffs was that "the process of environmental licensing of Highway BA – 099 took place despite the provision of ILO Convention 169 and Normative Instruction no. 184/2008 of IBAMA, given that the entrepreneurs neglected to perform mandatory stages of this procedure". Furthermore, they added that all consultations took place after the start of the construction work. The anticipated tutelage required, in the first instance, (paralyzing construction work and licensing), there was an appeal to this decision in which the anticipated tutelage was granted in order to:

> 'determine the immediate halt of the execution of construction work on the new Highway BA-099 and, consequently, any act regarding the enterprise, until the completion of the process of landhold regularization of the remaining community from the Quingoma quilombo, as well as until the completion of the necessary steps for environmental licensing of the enterprise related to the appearance of the environmental impact study by the intervening organ (Palmares Cultural Foundation), and the Prior, Free, and Informed Consultation with the traditional communities of Quingoma de Dentro, under the recommended terms of, respectively, Article 21 of Normative Instruction n. 184, IBAMA and ILO Convention 169."

It was the above decision that gave rise to STA 856, here examined. The appellants maintained that the issue raised before the Federal Supreme Court involved constitutional matters, because it requires the acknowledgement of Articles 216, 225, caput and Paragraph 1°, IV, 231, and Article 68 of the ADCT of the Federal Constitution, and in addition, that the works do not negatively impact the quilombola community's territory, and that the "*Bahia Norte Concessionaire had then carried out a public meeting on 3 September 2014 to present the project to the Quingoma community and other impacted people...*" It also adds that "the prior license [would have been] issued only in October 2014 – that is, after Prior Consultation with the community concerned".

Finally, it puts forward that the RFC 1's decision "implies serious damage to the economic and social order", for the construction work was already 80% concluded and that "paralyzing it would engender an inverse *periculum in mora* [danger in delay] and high material costs". It informs that "in only one month, the loss will add up to approximately R$15.828.125,00 (fifteen million, eight hundred and twenty eight thousand, one hundred and twenty five reais), and after one year of paralyzed activities the loss would amount to about R$46.000.000,00 (forty six million reais)".

To resolve the issue, Minister Carmen Lúcia alluded to the appealed decision, which was worded as follows:

> "In effect, as stated in the aggravated decision itself, the environmental licensing of the works described in the case files was carried out without Prior Consultation with the aforementioned people of the quilombola community, which is a manifested affront to the provisions of Article 6, item 1 and 2, of the aforementioned ILO Resolution (sic) 169, which states as follows:
>
> It can be seen that the aforementioned environmental licensing manifests as null and void, evidently, due to the lack of compliance with the referenced provisions, of which the aggravated decision did not dismiss any grounds
>
> It should be duly noted that the aforementioned ILO Convention 169 is applicable in the event dealt with in these case files, in the terms of its Articles 1 and 3, sections I and II of Decree no. 6.040/2007, which instituted the National Policy for the Sustainable Development of Traditional Peoples and Communities (...)
>
> It should also be noted that, the circumstance of the referred community supposedly being consulted about the work in question does not have the capacity to make up for the pointed omission, inasmuch as, as was well pointed out by the specialist in the Federal Public Ministry, "the promotion of hearings did not have the intention to substantially comply with the requirements of the aforementioned ILO Convention 169, since it did not seek to discuss the project in advance, to consider the feasibility of such implementation on that location, as well as to evaluate any changes

to be considered before the beginning of the work. Thus, as they proceeded, the entrepreneurs neglected the social, cultural, and environmental impact to be felt by the Quingoma Community.'

From the above declaration, the SFC understood that the object of the STA was limited to the analysis of meeting the requirements of 'Convention 169 on indigenous and tribal peoples', of the International Labour Organization – ILO, "for the alleged offense to Articles 216, 225, and 231 of the Constitution of the Republic and to Article 8 of the Transitional Constitutional Provisions Act is only of a reflexive manner'. Thus, the STA was not acknowledged, and the decision of the Federal Regional Court of the First Region was maintained.

Not acknowledging the STA, from a practical standpoint, implies honoring the RFC 1's decision and, consequently, puts into effect the provisions of Convention 169 regarding Consultation. However, it seems evident that the topic is of a constitutional nature, especially given the content of Paragraph 2 of Article 5 of the Federal Constitution, whereby the rights and guarantees expressed in the Constitution do not exclude others from the regime or principles it adopts, *or from international treaties* which the Federative Republic of Brazil is part of. Moreover, as we have already seen here, the South American Constitutional Courts have a tendency to consider that the rights contained in Convention 169 are constitutional in nature.

3.3 The Superior Court of Justice

The Superior Court of Justice is a superior court whose main mission is to unify the application and understanding of National Law (Federal Constitution Art. 195, III, a, b, and c) of an infra-constitutional nature and, as such, has received several appeals related to the application of Convention 169 and to the Consultation it stipulates. The matters submitted to the Superior Court of Justice, albeit under the mantle of infra-constitutionality, are very similar to those handled by the Supreme Federal Court, reaching the court though similar ways – as claims to revoke injunctions (or similarly) issued by lower courts.

The Superior Court of Justice, by dispatch of its then president Minister Felix Fischer, in Safety and Injunction Suspension SLS 1.745/PA conditioned the granting of an environmental license for the São Luiz do Tapajós Hydroelectric Power Plant on a Prior Consultation with all communities, indigenous or tribal, that were likely to be affected by the implementation of the enterprise, under the terms of ILO Convention 169. However, the Federal Public Ministry filed a Complaint[176] in court on the grounds that more than eight months after the legal decision, the measure had not yet been implemented. The defendant parties, especially the Unions, alleged they had been adopting measures to comply with the decision and, particularly, to allow for the discussion of a proposal to carry out a consultation process with the leaders of the Munduruku people about the hydraulic power harnessing in the Tapajós region. They added that in 2012 a Interministerial Working Group (GTI) was created to regulate the ILO Convention, in addition to a Specific Working Group (GT Tapajós). However, "it has not yet been possible to come to an agreement with the indigenous representatives concerning a participatory consultation process". The summary of the Court's decision was:

> A few months after the granting of the suspensive appeal (SLS n. 1.745/PA) which guaranteed the participation of indigenous and tribal communities potentially affected by the construction of an hydroelectric energy enterprise, before the concession of any environmental license, even if without a stipulated and definite term, it is not offensive to the authority of the aforementioned rule, since the effectiveness of this right is preserved, according to ILO Convention 169 (ratified by Decree no. 5.051/04) and the environmental principle of community participation (popular or citizen).

The minister reporting the decision also added that:

> As outlined in the monocratic decision I declared in SLS 1.745/PA, it is not possible to "start the execution of the enterprise without the communities involved manifesting themselves and contributing

[176] AgRg in Complaint no. 17.224- PA (2014/0062484-0).

> to the participatory process with their considerations regarding the enterprise that may directly affect them".
>
> Let us not forget that holding public consultations with indigenous and tribal peoples, as a means of pluralizing the corresponding political-administrative decision, in addition to the lack of necessary legal regulation, is not a simple task.
>
> According to information provided by the Union, the Government has been making efforts – and must indeed make progress – to start an effective dialogue with the peoples concerned, and allow for a wide debate on the enterprise, its economic and social importance for the country and possible negative impacts of different orders.
>
> The information provided by the Union verifies that "On 29 October 2013, based on the plea presented by the Pusuru Association, a new round of dialogue was held with indigenous leaders. The Federal Government financed the travel of the leaders to Brasilia so that they could participate in the meetings" (fl. 209)
>
> Furthermore, feasibility studies on energetic use are still under way, there is no EIA/RIMA protocol at IBAMA.
>
> It should be noted, however, that there is a need for the Federal Government to persist in its task of carrying out a comprehensive Prior Consultation with all indigenous and tribal peoples potentially affected by the energetic enterprise that is intended to be implemented, without which the environmental license will become unviable.

The decision originally delivered in AgRg in SLS 1754/PA[177] defined that:

> [a] ILO Convention 169 expressly determines in Article 6 that interested indigenous and tribal peoples must be consulted "whenever consideration is being given to legislative or administrative measures which may affect them directly". Nevertheless, carrying out mere preliminary studies that only relate to the feasibility of implementing the São Luiz do Tapajós/PA Hydroelectric Power Plant, doesn't have the power to directly affect

[177] Superior Tribunal of Justice. AgRg in SLS 1745 / PA, Rapporteur Minister Félix Fischer, Special Court, DJe 26/06/2013.

the indigenous communities involved. And moreso,: '...it is not possible to start the execution of the enterprise without the communities involved manifesting themselves and contributing to the participatory process of decision making'.

The decision seems right to us, for it protected the Indigenous Land from the project's impacts, though it did not prevent the Administration from making preliminary studies related to the enterprise's viability. Nonetheless, any measure that implies decision making regarding the actual implementation of the activity, under the terms of the decision, would necessarily have to be preceded by the Consultation process with the potentially impacted communities concerned. It is important to reaffirm that Consultation is a process, not a mere formal meeting, so by beginning the activities of informing and obtaining the opinion of indigenous peoples on a given project, the Consultation is already in progress and, as a dynamic process, it will only end with the completion of the enterprise in question.

3.4 The Federal Regional Court of the First Region

Even though the object of this study is the decisions handed down by the higher courts, we cannot overlook that the Federal Regional Court of the First Region, due to the great amount of deeds and its vast jurisdictional basis, plays a fundamental role in forming the understanding of higher courts, especially the Superior Court of Justice. The Federal Regional Court of the First Region has been deciding on numerous matters since the incorporation of Convention 169 into domestic law. However, these decisions seem to be interpreting the provisions of Convention 169 in a very particular and, frankly, maximalist manner. The standard that has been adopted in some decisions has no parallel in the average jurisprudence of the South American Constitutional Courts. Note that in the case of port works carried out in the Amazon, the Federal Regional Court of the First Region understood that, in addition to other matters related to the venture:

'it also wasn't preceded by a regular prior consultation with the remaining peoples of the quilombola communities and other traditional populations in riverbanks, directly affected, which at first characterized the irregularity of the enterprise, to authorizing the suspension of the mentioned license in order to avoid irreversible damage or difficult or uncertain reparation, as in this case'[178]

The South American constitutional jurisprudence, amply presented above, shows us that even though the Consultation is a legal determination and a right of indigenous and tribal peoples, it doesn't have the power to imply, almost automatically, the paralysis of administrative activities in casein case it hasn't been applied, except in exceptional cases. Let us recall the following excerpts of the decision delivered by the Peruvian Constitutional Court (Exp. no. 0022-2009-PI/TC).

24. From the reading of Articles 6 and 15 of Convention 169 it is not apparent that indigenous peoples have a kind of right of veto. That is, the State's obligation of consulting indigenous peoples regarding legislative or administrative measures that may directly affect them doesn't grant them the capacity to prevent such measures from coming into effect.

In practice, the Federal Regional Court of the First Region bestowed the right of veto to traditional communities by determining the interruption of the environmental licensing procedure. The above decision, the excerpt of which was transcribed, follows the gist of another previous one, in which appears:

"for the implementation of the Naval Pole in the state of Amazonas, it is necessary to comply with supra-legal norms – ILO Convention 169, the Convention on Biological Diversity, and the Universal Declaration on Cultural Diversity, of which the country is a signatory –; constitutional norms – Article 215 Paragraph 1, 216, 231, and 232 –; and infra-constitutional norms referring to the protection of the rights of traditional populations. ...The absence of

[178] Federal Regional Court of the First Region. AG 0027843-13.2016.4.01.0000 / PA; Rapporteur Federal Judge Souza Prudente, 5th Panel, Publication: 24/05/2017 e-DJF1. Decision: 03/05/2017.

> prior and free consultation and clear consent from the traditional communities involved in the expropriation process makes the implementation illegal and illegitimate."[179]

The jurisprudence of the Third Panel of the Court apparently does not apply Convention 169 in a 'flexible' way, since it deals with Consultation as an absolute right, without realizing it is a process and not a rigidly defined moment in time, as if it were a mere public hearing to be carried out within the p environmental licensing procedure. The plain and simple interruption of a licensing process doesn't not bring concrete gains for any of the involved parties and, ultimately, can lead to losses for all of them.

Nevertheless, through means of internal resources, the Special Court of the Federal Regional Court of the First Region[180] has positively valorized the economic threat to enterprises caused by interruptions resulting from the concession of anticipated protective measures, suspending decisions of a paralyzing nature for the licensing processes. In effect, there was a suspension of the effects of the tutelage granted by a judgement in a first lower court with the purpose of ordering that a Prior, Free, and Informed Consultation be made with the indigenous peoples Kayabi, Munduruku, and Apiaká, potentially affected by the hydroelectric power plant of São Manoel, to be built on the Teles Pires river, located between the states of Mato Grosso and Pará. The Court found that stopping the licensing process of the dam was capable of causing:

> "severe disturbance to the administrative order and the public economy due to the serious and well-founded risk of losing the so-called hydrological window (dry season), which would have to be moved to the following year, resulting in the complete paralysis of the construction and assembly works of the power plant, thus

[179] Federal Regional Court of the First Region. AG 0031507-23.2014.4.01.0000 / AM; Rapporteur Federal Judge Ney Bello, 3rd Panel, Publication: 12/06/2015 e-DJF1 P. 3172. Date of Decision: 09/06/2015.

[180] Appeal 00559382420144010000, Rapporteur Federal Judge Hilton Queiroz. Special Court. e-DJF1: 22/11/2016.

> making the production of energy no longer viable in the stipulated schedule (March/2018)."

In fact, it should be noted that the Consultation of Convention 169 is not to be confused with the public hearing process of environmental licensing, although it is possible to take advantage of some parts of the environmental hearing and, particularly, assume good faith in the licensing process.

In another case, the National Agency of Oil, Natural Gas, and Biofuels filed an appeal with the Federal Regional Court of the First Region[181] against the decision of the Single Judicial District of the Cruzeiro do Sul/AC Judicial Subsection, which granted a request for the anticipation of the protective effects formulated in the records of the Public Civil Action proposed by the Federal Public Ministry, in which the legality of offering blocks for the exploitation of hydrocarbons in the Sedimentary Basin of Acre was discussed, whether of conventional or non-conventional resources. Here, two main issues were under discussion: (i) the need to carry out an Environmental Evaluation of the Sedimentary Area (AAAS) and (ii) to carry out a Prior Consultation process with indigenous peoples and traditional populations potentially affected by the projects to be implemented in the blocks' areas offered in the bid. Regarding the issue of Prior Consultation specifically, the Court found that:

> "ILO Convention 169, in its Article 6, determines that Governments must, every time legislative or administrative measures that may directly affect traditional populations are foreseen, promote consultation with the peoples concerned, through the proper procedures. (...) Although, in this case, there is no overlap of indigenous lands and the area of offered blocks and therefore, about area AC-T-8, the above data determined by FUNAI reveals that the exploitation of non-conventional gas authorized by the ANP bidding would not be very distant from some of the indigenous lands located in the Acre Basin, so that it becomes absolutely evident, and crystalclear, how indigenous interests would be directly affected by

[181] Federal Regional Court of the First Region. APPEAL 00084674120164010000. Rapporteur FEDERAL JUDGE JIRAIR ARAM MEGUERIAN. Publication: 10/05/2016.

the exploitation of shale gas. In the particular case of Block AC-T-8, when analyzing the map of indigenous lands on page 9 and comparing it to the map of offered areas by the ANP in Acre (page 87), we can see that this block is too close to at least three indigenous lands, Nukini, Nawa, and Payanawa. As for the illustration on page 391, an annexed part of a scientific study, it is possible to observe the proximity to the indigenous land of Vale do Jari, plaintiff of the repudiation note on pages 06-16 - Annex I. *However, there was no consultation with the indigenous population in the region to be exploited, with several documents in the records that show a great concern of the indians regarding fracking activities close to their lands* (...). When the aforementioned Convention establishes that there must be a consultation with 'peoples concerned', it means it must be directed to any population that may in some way, directly or indirectly, even minimally, be affected by the activity to be carried out. (...) On this matter, ILO Convention 169 is quite clear, mentioning that this consultation with the indians must be made 'before undertaking or permitting any programmes' (art. 15, paragraph 2). (...) very well. The absence of prior consultation, along the lines mentioned above, with traditional populations, was made evident during the civil investigation carried out by the FPM (...)" 12. Therefore, the contested decision does not deserve amendments, because the aggravating factor didn't succeed in deconstituting the relevant foundations adopted in said aggravated decision, based on robust documents, so that detailed analysis of possible evidence or technical expertise appears to be necessary, to verify the actual location of the exploitation and its distance from indigenous lands or the occurrence, or not, of overlap of the exploitation area with the legally protected areas, as well as the real environmental impact on the region."

The above decision, just as the previous one, adopts a maximalist conception of the role of Consultation, giving it power that, as we have seen, doesn't correspond to the findings of the South-American Constitutional Courts, notably in cases in which the ownership of natural resources belongs to the State, as is the case with the hydrocarbons.

Conclusion

After analyzing the entire development of this work, the reader may come to different conclusions regarding the addressed subject. The first conclusion that surfaces is that the matter is here to stay and that it is definitively incorporated into the context of Human Rights. Certainly, in many countries in South America, Convention 169 possesses constitutional dignity, since its provisions are integrated into the register of fundamental rights.

Consultation, which is mentioned in Convention 169 seven times, is a general clause that aims to achieve an agreement between the parties involved in a given project. It must be carried out with the *peoples concerned* [Article 6 (1)(a)]. The people *concerned* are the community that is *directly* or *indirectly* affected by the project in question. However, we cannot disconsider the level of influence of the project upon the people concerned. In effect, the normative force of the Consultation must be proportional to the level of impact on the community. It is important to observe that indirect repercussions tend to involve a higher degree of subjectivity than directly measurable consequences. Therefore, communities that are indirectly affected cannot, in the context of a Consultation, be attributed the same relevance as communities that suffer direct repercussions, so that the negative burden suffered by the community that endures the direct impact of a project or enterprise is not diminished.

One aspect that cannot be neglected is related to the administrative and/or legislative measures that may affect indigenous and tribal peoples. Interesting issues arise here. First of all, legislative measures (*rectius*: laws) are in principle generic and tend to affect the entire population of a given country. Therefore, it seems quite reasonable that, when it comes to general laws that affect the entire population of a certain country, there is no need to speak of Consultation, Agreement, or Consent of indigenous and tribal peoples. However, in the case of measures with direct repercussions on indigenous or tribal peoples – on their lifestyle as much as on their territory – Consultation is pertinent and mandatory, according to the terms of Convention 169. In such cases, both the Legislative and the Executive Power must provide the means so that the affected communities (effectively or potentially) can express their opinions about the project in question. This opinion, however, is not binding to the Administration, nor to the Legislative Power, since the Convention doesn't stipulate this. Thus, in the case of administrative or legislative measures, there is a duty to take into consideration the opinion expressed by indigenous and tribal peoples, but this doesn't imply an obligation to adopt the standpoints expressed in the Consultation. Likewise, it seems correct to state that the choice of not adopting the measures suggested in the Consultation must be motivated and founded, so that the reasons become clear to those concerned.

Consultation must be carried out in good faith and in a manner appropriate to the circumstances. This means that there is no formula for conducting the Consultation, since good faith and the appropriate way are open concepts to be given meaning on a case by case basis. Although the legal concept of good will can't be affirmed, it is certainly possible to identify bad willed behaviour, Behaviours that indicate bad will in negotiations include offering jobs to community leaders or their relatives, and presenting incomplete, truncated, or false information.. The appropriate way is certainly the way that doesn't harm the culture of the peoples concerned.

Consultation is a dynamic procedure that must be part of the entire lifespan of the project or enterprise, its implementation cannot be used up, that is, throughout the lifespan of the enterprise – as well as its demobilization – it is necessary that the entrepreneur and community keep an open dialogue about the development of actions and their repercussions on the community.

Article 6 extensively makes use of the term Consultation, for example: (1) (a) 'consult the peoples concerned'; (2) 'The consultations carried out ...with the objective of achieving agreement or consent to the proposed measure'; likewise, Article 15 employs the same term when it deals with the exploitation of minerals in indigenous lands that are state property, in such a case the Consultation aims to "consult these peoples, with a view to ascertaining whether and to what degree their interests would be prejudiced, before undertaking or permitting any programmes for the exploration or exploitation of such resources pertaining to their lands". Clearly, in this case Consultation doesn't have the power to prevent an activity, it is limited to being an instrument – of extreme relevance, in fact – to determine whether indigenous interests will be harmed and to what extent. Reading the final part of the article makes us aware that the case is one of indemnity and/or compensation and not of paralysis or veto against the enterprise: "The peoples concerned shall wherever possible participate in the benefits of such activities, and shall receive fair compensation for any damages which they may sustain as a result of such activities."

The case of Consent considered in Article 16 is completely different. It deals with an extreme situation in which the indigenous or tribal peoples must be displaced from their natural traditional habitat. The relocation of indigenous peoples can only take place after completing adequate procedures established by national legislation, including public surveys, when appropriate, in which the peoples concerned have the possibility of being effectively represented. Once the transfer has been carried out, and when the necessity has abated, Article 16 (3) states, 'whenever possible, these peoples shall have the right to return to their traditional lands.'

The right to Consultation doesn't induce a right to veto projects and investment programmes, for this is not the goal of Convention 169, whose fundamental character is to serve as an instrument for the improvement of intercultural dialogue that must be permanent, so that indigenous claims are treated as a high priority by the Public Administration.

References

Books and Articles

ACSELRAD, Henri; MELLO, Cecília Campello do Amaral and BEZERRA, Gustavo das Neves. **O que é Justiça Ambiental**. Rio de Janeiro: Garamond, 2009.

ALENCAR, José de. **O guarani**. São Paulo: Ática, 20th ed., 1996.

ALMEIDA, Maria Regina Celestino de. Catequese, **Aldeamentos e Missionação**, in, FRAGOSO, João and GOUVEA, Maria de Fátima (editors), **Coleção Brasil Colônia, I (1443-1580)**. 2014, pp 435-478.

ALMEIDA, Maria Regina Celestino de. **Os Índios na História do Brasil**, Rio de Janeiro: Fundação Getúlio Vargas, 2010.

ALMEIDA, Rita Heloisa de. **O Diretório dos Índios – Um projeto de "Civilização" no Brasil do Século XVIII**. Brasília: Editora da Universidade de Brasília, 1997.

ANAYA, S. James. **International Human Rights and Indigenous Peoples**, New York: Aspen Publishers, 2009.

ANTUNES, Paulo de Bessa. **Direito Ambiental**, São Paulo: Atlas, 19ªth edition, 2017.

______. **Uma Nova Introdução ao Direito,** Rio de Janeiro: Renovar, 2nd edition, 1992.

BACCI, Massimo Livi. **Conquista – A destruição dos Índios Americanos.** (Translation Sandra Escobar). Lisbon: Edições 70. 2007.

BANDEIRA, Maria de Lourdes. **Terras Negras: invisibilidade expropriadora**, in, Textos e Debates, Year 1, no. 2, 1991, UFSC, pp 7-23.

BANTON, Michael. **A Ideia de Raça** (Translation by António Marques Bessa), Lisbon, Edições 70, 2015.

CARVALHO, Guilherme. **Os Bancos Multilaterais e o Complexo Rio Madeira: A tentativa de garantir o controle dos recursos naturais da Amazônia para o grande capital**, in, CEDI - Centro Ecumênico de Documentação e Informação - **Povos indí-ge-nas no Brasil** - 1987/88/89/90, *Aconteceu*, spe-cial no. 18, São Paulo, 1991, p. 29.

CIDH. **Derechos de los pueblos indígenas y tribales sobre sus tierras ancestrales y recursos naturales. Normas y jurisprudencia del Sistema Interamericano de Derechos Humanos**. December 2009, OEA/Ser. L/V/II. Doc. 56/09, párr. 333.

Committee on The Elimination of Racial Discrimination, 87th Session (2015) by The Association of Indigenous Village Leaders in Suriname. The Association of Saramaka Authorities/ The Forest Peoples Programme. A Report on the Situation of Indigenous and Tribal Peoples In Suriname and Comments on Suriname's 13th- 15th Periodic Reports (CERD/C/SUR/13-15) 14 July 2015.

CONTESSE, Jorge and LOVERA, Domingo. **El Convenio 169 de la OIT en la jurisprudencia chilena: prólogo del incumplimiento**, in, Anuario de Derecho Público 2011, Santiago: Universidad Diego Portales.
COSTA, João Batista de Almeida and OLIVEIRA, Cláudia Luz (editors). **Cerrado, Gerais, Sertão - Comunidades Tradicionais nos Sertões Roseanos**, São Paulo: Intermeios, 2012.

Cultural Survival, Quarterly, 10.2 (Summer 1986) Land Rights: Strategies for Survival

CUNHA, Manuela Carneiro da. **Índios no Brasil (História, Direitos e Cidadania)**, São Paulo: Claro Enigma, 2012.

CUNHA, Manuela Carneiro da. ***Os Direitos do Índio***, São Paulo: Brasiliense, 1987.

DAVIS, Shelton H. **The World Bank and Indigenous Peoples**, The World Bank, 1993.

DEROCHE, Frédéric. **La Notion de "peuples autochtones, une synthèse des principaux débats terminologiques,** in, FRITZ, Jean Claude; DEROCHE, Frédéric; FRITZ, Gérard and PORTEILLA, Raphäel (sous la direction de). **La Nouvelle Question Indigène.** Paris: L` Harmattan, 2005.

DIAMOND, Jared. **Colapso – Como as Sociedades Escolhem o Fracasso ou o Sucesso** (Translation by Alexandre Raposo). Rio de Janeiro: Record, 2005.

DIAS, Simone Conceição Soares, **Trajetória dos Fundos de Pasto na Bahia**, in, ANAIS ELETRÔNICOS - VI Encontro Estadual de História - ANPUH/BAHIA, 2013.

DOROUGH, Dalee Sambo. **The Revision of International Labour Organization Convention no. 107: a subjective assessment,** in, DUNBAR-ORTIZ, Roxanne; DOROUGH, Dalee Sambo, ALFREDSSON, Gudmundur; SWEPSTON, Lee and WILLE, Petter (Edited by), **Indigenous Peoples' Rights In International Law: Emergence and application - Book in honor of Asbjørn Eide at eighty.** Kautokeino & Copenhagen: Gáldu & IWGIA, 2015.

DOYLE, Cathal M. **Indigenous Peoples, Title to territory, Rights and Resources – The transformative role of free prior and informed consent.** London and New York: Routledge. 2015.

DUE PROCESS OF LAW FOUNDATION [DPLF], **Digesto de jurisprudencia latinoamericana sobre los derechos de los pueblos indígenas a la participación, la consulta previa y la propiedad comunitaria,** Washington, 2013.

FAUSTO, Carlos. **Os índios antes do Brasil**, 2014, Zahar, Rio de Janeiro, Zahar, 4th reprint.

FEARNSIDE, P.M. 1987. **Frenesi de Desmatamento no Brasil: A Floresta Amazônica Irá Sobreviver?** pp. 45-57 In: G. Kohlhepp and A. Schrader (eds.) **Homem e Natureza na Amazônia.** Tübinger Geographische Studien 95 (Tübinger Beiträge zur Geographischen Lateinamerika-Forschung 3). Geographisches Institut, Universität Tübingen, Tübingen, Germany.

FRASER, Nancy and HONNETH, Axel, **Redistribution or Recognition – A Political-Philosophical Exchange.** Verso, London-New York. 2003.

GALVIS, Maria Clara and RAMIREZ, Angela. **Manual para defender os direitos dos povos indígenas** (tradução Rodolfo Marinho), Washington: Due Process of Law Foundation, s/d.

GANDAVO, Pedro de Magalhães. **Tratado da Terra do Brasil e a História da Província de Santa Cruz**, Kindle Edition, 1574 (2014).

GARCIA, Rodolfo. **Ensaio sobre a História Política e Administrativa do Brasil (1500-1810).** Rio de Janeiro: José Olympio/INL, 2nd Edition, 1975.

GOMES, Flávio dos Santos. **Mocambos e Quilombos – Uma História do Campesinato Negro no Brasil.** São Paulo: Claroenigma, 2015.

GOODLAND, Robert. **Free, Prior and Informed Consent and the World Bank Group.** Sustainable Development Law and Policy, Summer 2004, 66-74.

GRIFFITHS, Tom, **Indigenous peoples and the World Bank: experiences with participation, Indigenous Peoples Program.** Forests Peoples Program: Moreton-in-Marsh, 2005.

Grupo de Trabajo Asuntos Indígenas de la ULA, Provea, Laboratorio de Paz: Lexys Rendón Situación del **Derecho a la Consulta Previa en Venezuela.** Caracas. 2016.

HALL, Gilbert and PATRINOS, Anthony, **Latin America`s Indigenous Peoples, Finance and Development,** December 2005, Volume 42, Number 4.

HANNIGAN, John. **Environmental Sociology**, London and New York: Routledge, 3rd edition. 2014.

HESPANHA, António Manuel. **O Caleidoscópio do Direito – O Direito e a Justiça no Mundo de Hoje,** Coimbra, Almedina, 2nd Edition (reprint), 2014.

HOLANDA, Sérgio Buarque de. **História Geral da Civilização Brasileira, 1 – A época colo-nial (do des-co-bri-men-to à expan-são ter-ri-to-rial).** São Paulo: DIFEL, 7th Edition, 1985.

HOLANDA, Sérgio Buarque de. **História Geral da Civilização Brasileira – Tomo I – A Época Colonial, Volume I – Do Descobrimento à Expansão territorial**, Rio de Janeiro: Bertrand Brasil, 13th edition, 2003.

Indigenous Peoples, October 2016

INTERNATIONAL WORK GROUP FOR INDIGENOUS AFFAIRS (IWGIA), The **Indigenous World 2016,** Copenhagen. 2016.

KAMBEL, Ellen-Rose and MACKAY, Fergus Copenhagen: IWGIA, 1999.

LACERDA, Rosane Freire. **A Convenção 169 da OIT sobre Povos Indígenas e Tribais: Origem, Conteúdo e Mecanismos de Supervisão e Aplicação.** S/d.

M´BOKOLO, Elikia. **África negra – História e Civilizações. Tomo I** (até o século **XVIII**), Salvador: EDUFBA – Casa das Áfricas, 2009 .

MACKAY, Fergus. **A guide to indigenous peoples` rights in the Inter-American Human Rights System.** Copenhagen: IWGIA, 2002.

MAIA, Luciano Mariz. **Legislação Indigenista**, Brasília: Senado Federal, 1993.

MARTINS JR., Izidoro. **História do Direito Nacional**, Brasília: Ministério da Justiça, 1979.

McANANY, Patricia A. and YOFFEE, Norman (Edited by). **Questioning Collapse – Human Resilience, Ecological Vulnerability, and the Aftermath of Empire.** New York: Cambridge University Press, 2012.

MENDES JÚNIOR, João. **Os Indígenas do Brazil, seus Direitos Individuaes e Políticos** (Edição Fac-Similar), São Paulo: Typ. Hennies Irmãos, 1912.

MENDONÇA, Marcos Carneiro de. **Raízes da Formação Administrativa do Brasil**, tomo I, Instituto Histórico e Geográfico Brasileiro/Conselho Federal de Cultura, 1972.

MORAN, Emilio. **Nós e a Natureza** (Translation by Carlos Szlak), São Paulo: SENAC, 2008.

MOREIRA, Adriano. **Tratado de Tordesilhas de 7 de junho de 1494**, in, Nação e Defesa, Year XIX, no. 70, April - June 1994, Instituto de Defesa Nacional, Lisbon, pp 9 -25.

NISKIER, Gustavo. **Conflitos indígenas e projetos de desenvolvimento econômico.** Master Dissertation. PUC/RJ, p. 18, in http://www.urb.puc-rio.br/dissertacao/dissertacao_gustavo_niskier.pdf, Accessed on 25/11/2017.

OIT. **La aplicación del convenio núm. 169 por tribunales nacionales e internacionales en América Latina: una compilación de casos.** Ginebra: OIT, 2009.

OLIVEIRA, João Pacheco de. **Os indígenas na fundação da colônia**, in, FRAGOSO, João and GOUVEA, Maria de Fátima (editors), **Coleção Brasil Colônia, I (1443-1580)**. pp 167-228. 2014.

PATINO, Maria Clara Galvis and RINCÓN, Ángela Mari Ramirez (2013), **Digesto de jurisprudencia latinoamericana sobre los derechos de los pueblos indígenas a la participación, la consulta previa y la propiedad comunitaria**, Washington: Fundación para el Debido Proceso, 2013.

PEREIRA, Osny Duarte. **Direito Florestal Brasileiro,** Rio de Janeiro: Borsoi, 1950.

Pontes de Miranda - **Comentários à Constituição de 1946, vol. V,** Rio de Janeiro: Max Limonad. 1953.

Pontes de Miranda. **Comentários à Constituição da República dos E.U. do Brasil.** Rio de Janeiro: Editora Guanabara Waissmann, Koogan Ltda. Tomo II. 1937.

PRICE, Richard. **Maroon Societies: Rebel Slave Communities in the Americas** (Edited by), New York: Anchor Book, 1973, Kindle Edition.

Princípios do Equador, **Os Princípios do Equador III, um referencial do setor financeiro para identificação, avaliação e gerenciamento de riscos socioambientais em projetos,** June 2013.

PROENÇA, Maria Cândida. **Uma História Concisa de Portugal.** Lisbon: Círculo de Leitores. 2015.

RAMOS, Alcida Rita. **Sociedades Indígenas,** São Paulo: Ática, 1986..

ROJAS, Biviany Garzón; YAMADA, Erika M and OLIVEIRA, Rodrigo. **Direito à consulta e consentimento de povos indígenas, quilombolas e comunidades tradicionais.** São Paulo : Rede de Cooperação Amazônica - RCA ; Washington, DC : Due Process of Law Foundation, 2016.

ROMBOUTS, S.J. **Having a Say – Indigenous Peoples, International Law and Free, Prior and Informed Consent.** Oisterwijk: Wolf Legal Publishers. 2014.

ROULAN, Norbert (editor), PIERRÉ-CAPS, Stéphanie and POUMARÈDE, Jacques. **Direito das minorias e Povos Autóctones** (Translation by Ane Lize Spaltemberg). 2004. Brasíla: Unb.

RUIZ, Rafael. **Francisco de Vitoria e os direitos dos índios americanos – a evolução da legislação indígena castelhana no século XVI.** Porto Alegre: EDIPUCRS, 2002.

TAMANG, Parshuram. **An Overview of the Principle of Free, Prior and Informed Consent and Indigenous Peoples in International and Domestic Law and Practices.** DEPARTMENT OF ECONOMIC AND SOCIAL AFFAIRS, Division for Social Policy and Development, Secretariat of the Permanent Forum on Indigenous Issues, WORKSHOP ON FREE, PRIOR AND INFORMED CONSENT (New York, 17-19 January 2005).

TARAGÓ, Myriam Noemi. **Los Pueblos Originarios y La Conquista.** 1st Edition. Buenos Aires: Sudamericana, Kindle Edition. 2014.

WAINER, Ann Helen. **Legislação Ambiental do Brasil (Subsídios para a História do Direito Ambiental).** Rio de Janeiro: Forense, 1991.

WITKOSKI, Antônio Carlos. **Terras, Florestas e Águas de Trabalho**. São Paulo: Annablume, 2nd edition, s/d.

WORLD Bank, **Emerging** MERGING LESSONS SERIES NO. 2 | The Inspection Panel.

Websites

- http://ajurisprudencia.tcpbolivia.bo/jurisprudencia/envio/envio contenido.php?fnombres=consulta%20previa&tiposentencia=0& tiporecurso=0
- http://ajurisprudencia.tcpbolivia.bo/jurisprudencia/envio/envio contenido.php?fnombres=consulta%20previa&tiposentencia=0& tiporecurso=0
- http://cidh.org/countryrep/TierrasIndigenas2009/Cap.IX.htm#,
- http://coleccion.educ.ar/coleccion/CD18/contenidos/informaci on/leyes/constituciones/cp_chaco.pdf
- http://coleccion.educ.ar/coleccion/CD18/contenidos/informaci on/leyes/constituciones/cp_chaco.pdf
- http://decs.pjud.cl/index.php/tendencias

- http://infojusnoticias.gov.ar/opinion/la-corte-suprema-y-el-derecho-a-la-consulta-de-los-pueblos-indigenas-144.html
- http://infojusnoticias.gov.ar/opinion/la-corte-suprema-y-el-derecho-a-la-consulta-de-los-pueblos-indigenas-144.html
- http://latinoamericana.wiki.br/verbetes/p/plano-colombia
- http://linux.an.gov.br/mapa/?p=4843,
- http://nacoesunidas.org/conheca/paises-membros/
- http://pdba.georgetown.edu/Constitutions/Bolivia/boli via09.html
- http://pdba.georgetown.edu/Constitutions/Peru/per93reforms0 5.html
- http://philip.inpa.gov.br/publ_livres/Dossie/Mad/Outros%20d ocumentos/As%20IFMs%20e%20o%20Complexo%20Rio%20 Madeira.pdf
- http://servicios.infoleg.gob.ar/infolegInternet/anexos/0-4999/804/norma.htm
- http://servicios.infoleg.gob.ar/infolegInternet/anexos/45000-49999/46871/norma.htm
- http://www.acnur.org/t3/fileadmin/Documentos/Pueblos_indig enas/ley_organica_indigena_ven.pdf
- http://www.bancomundial.org/es/about/history
- http://www.cjf.jus.br/juris/unificada,
- http://www.constitution.org/cons/argentin.htm
- http://www.corteconstitucional.gov.co/inicio/Constitucion%20 politica%20de%20Colombia%20-%202015.pdf
- http://www.corteconstitucional.gov.co/relatoria/1997/su039-97.htm,
- http://www.corteidh.or.cr/
- http://www.corteidh.or.cr/docs/casos/articulos/seriec_127_esp. pdf
- http://www.corteidh.or.cr/docs/casos/articulos/seriec_172_ing. pdf

- http://www.corteidh.or.cr/index.php/es/acerca-de/como-acceder-al-sistema-interamericano/denuncias-consultas,
- Http://www.cultura.gov.py/marcolegal/ley-90481-estatuto-de-las-comunidades-indigenas
- http://www.culturalsurvival.org/publications/cultural-survival-quarterly/brazil/warfare-polonoroeste,
- http://www.dplf.org/sites/default/files/digesto_indigenas_web_final.pdf
- http://www.ftierra.org/index.php/component/attachments/download/6
- http://www.imf.org/external/np/exr/facts/glance.htm
- http://www.iwgia.org/regiones/latin-america/argentina
- http://www.iwgia.org/regiones/latin-america/chile
- http://www.iwgia.org/regiones/latin-america/guatemala/64-esp-paises/bolivia/561-pueblos-indigenas-de-bolivia-hoy
- http://www.lexivox.org/norms/BO-L-3058.xhtml
- http://www.leychile.cl/Navegar?idNorma=30620
- http://www.mapuche.info/news02/tribuno010731.html
- http://www.mibolivia.net/36-etnias-de-bolivia-pueblos-indigenas/
- [1]http://www.mpf.mp.br/pa/sala-de-imprensa/documentos/2016/tabela_de_acompanhamento_belo_monte_atualizada_mar_2016.pdf/
- http://www.oas.org/es/acerca/quienes_somos.asp,
- http://www.oas.org/juridico/pdfs/mesicic4_ecu_const.pdf
- http://www.oas.org/juridico/PDFs/mesicic4_ecu_const.pdf
- http://www.oas.org/juridico/spanish/par_res3.htm
- http://www.oas.org/pt/cidh/mandato/que.asp
- http://www.oeco.org.br/reportagens/25872-estrada-pelo-tipnis-a-novela-continua/
- http://www.portaldeabogados.com.ar/portal/index.php/leyes/54-leyesnacion/231-16986-accion-de-amparo.html

- http://www.saij.gob.ar/corte-suprema-justicia-nacion-federal-ciudad-autonoma-buenos-aires-pilquiman-crecencio-instituto-autarquico-colonizacion-fomento-rural-accion-amparo-fa14000148-2014-10-07/123456789-841-0004-1ots-eupmocsollaf
- http://www.saij.gob.ar/corte-suprema-justicia-nacion-federal-ciudad-autonoma-buenos-aires-pilquiman-crecencio-instituto-autarquico-colonizacion-fomento-rural-accion-amparo-fa14000148-2014-10-07/123456789-841-0004-1ots-eupmocsollaf
- http://www.siise.gob.ec/siiseweb/PageWebs/glosario/ficglo_napuin.htm
- http://www.tbg.com.br/pt_br/o-gasoduto/tracado.htm
- http://www.tc.gob.pe/jurisprudencia/2011/00024-2009-AI.html
- http://www.territorioin, digenaygobernanza.com/bolivia.html
- http://www.territorioindigena.com.ar/Pueblos-Originarios
- http://www.urosario.edu.co/jurisprudencia/catedra-viva-intercultural/ur/Legislacion-colombiana-para-comunidades-etnicas/
- https://jurisprudencia.tcpbolivia.bo/
- https://pt.wikipedia.org/wiki/Quilombo#cite_note-20
- https://tc.gob.pe/jurisprudencia/2010/06316-2008-AA.pdf
- https://terrasindigenas.org.br/en/terras-indigenas/3835
- https://terrasindigenas.org.br/en/terras-indigenas/3835
- https://www.corteconstitucional.gob.ec/
- https://www.corteconstitucional.gob.ec/images/stories/pdfs/SUBE_Y_BAJA/SUBE_Y_BAJA3/Sentencia_mineros.pdf
- https://www.leychile.cl/Navegar?idNorma=1006486,
- https://www.leychile.cl/Navegar?idNorma=242302
- https://www.leychile.cl/Navegar?idNorma=30667
- https://www.oas.org/juridico/mla/sp/ven/sp_ven-int-const.html
- www.equatro-principles.com
- http://aempresarial.com/web/informativo.php?id=4049

- http://www.corteconstitucional.gov.co/relatoria/2009/C-175-09.htm,
- http://www.corteconstitucional.gov.co/relatoria/2012/T-376-12.htm,
- http://www.corteconstitucional.gov.co/relatoria/2003/su383-03.htm
- http://www.imf.org/external/pubs/ft/fandd/2005/12/hall.htm #author
- https://afros.files.wordpress.com/2008/08/mapa-afroecuatorianos1.jpg
- http://direitopublicoediversidade.blogspot.com.br/2009/12/con vencao-169-da-oit-sobre-povos.html
- http://14nacionalidadesy18gruposetnicos.blogspot.com.br/2013 /04/nacionalidades-y-pueblos-de-la-region.html
- http://anpuhba.org/wp-content/uploads/2013/12/Simone-Concei%C3%A7%C3%A3o-Soares-Dias.pdf
- http://g1.globo.com/economia/noticia/2016/04/belo-monte-inicia-operacao-comercial-6-anos-apos-ser-licitada.html
- http://www.palmares.gov.br/wp-content/uploads/2017/05/quadro-geral-15-05-2017.pdf
- https://aiatsis.gov.au/explore/articles/mabo-case

Made in the USA
Monee, IL
05 November 2026

68020979R00114